How to Mix Methods is a concise and accessible guide to the methodology. Katz-Buonincontro outlines the fundamentals clearly and engagingly for research methods students through numerous examples, intriguing metaphors, and detailed flowcharts. This state-of-the-art resource is a substantive contribution to the mixed methods literature.

—**Johnny Saldaña, MFA,** Professor Emeritus, Arizona State University, Phoenix, AZ, United States

This clear and well-planned-out book is a needed addition to all researchers' bookshelves who plan to conduct or are conducting mixed methods research! The book will assist in carrying out a rigorous mixed methods study and includes many excellent suggestions for overcoming challenges that may arise throughout a mixed methods study.

—**Nancy L. Leech, PhD,** Professor, University of Colorado Denver, Denver, CO, United States

As an experienced mixed methods researcher and mentor, I appreciate how this book concisely explains the design essentials. Its conversational tone and practical examples demystify the requisite integration of qualitative and quantitative research. Despite its brevity, this comprehensive introduction reflects contemporary mixed methods research practices, offering an accessible approach to enhancing research capacity and innovation.

—**Cheryl Poth, PhD,** Professor, University of Alberta, Edmonton, AB, Canada

HOW TO MIX METHODS

HOW TO MIX METHODS

A Guide to Sequential, Convergent, and Experimental Research Designs

JEN KATZ-BUONINCONTRO

 AMERICAN PSYCHOLOGICAL ASSOCIATION

Published by
American Psychological Association
750 First Street, NE
Washington, DC 20002
https://www.apa.org

Order Department
https://www.apa.org/pubs/books
order@apa.org

Typeset in Charter and Interstate by Circle Graphics, Inc., Reisterstown, MD

Printer: Gasch Printing, Odenton, MD
Cover Designer: Anne Kerns, Anne Likes Red, Inc., Silver Spring, MD

Library of Congress Cataloging-in-Publication Data

Names: Katz-Buonincontro, Jen, author.
Title: How to mix methods : a guide to sequential, convergent, and
  experimental research designs / authored by Jen Katz-Buonincontro.
Description: Washington, DC : American Psychological Association, [2024] |
  Includes bibliographical references and index.
Identifiers: LCCN 2023050952 (print) | LCCN 2023050953 (ebook) |
  ISBN 9781433840098 (paperback) | ISBN 9781433840104 (ebook)
Subjects: LCSH: Psychology--Research--Methodology. | BISAC: PSYCHOLOGY /
  Research & Methodology | SOCIAL SCIENCE / Research
Classification: LCC BF76.5 .K318 2024 (print) | LCC BF76.5 (ebook) |
  DDC 150.72/1--dc23/eng/20240205
LC record available at https://lccn.loc.gov/2023050952
LC ebook record available at https://lccn.loc.gov/2023050953

https://doi.org/10.1037/0000404-000

Printed in the United States of America

10 9 8 7 6 5 4 3 2 1

How to Mix Methods *is dedicated to Dr. Paul Goldman,*
my mentor and cochair of my doctoral studies.
With his kind, patient, and extremely supportive teaching
and mentoring, I was able to spark an interest in learning,
doing, and then teaching qualitative methods.
This later developed into a general love of research and
a desire to learn new methods, break through stigmas,
and land on this new planet of mixed methods research.
We miss you, Paul. I know the world was made a better place
with you, your ideas, and your mentoring of all your students . . .
though, I'd like to think, especially me.

Contents

List of Tables, Figures, and Exhibits

Acknowledgments

I'm exceptionally grateful for my husband Matt's enduring support as well as the encouragement from my kids, Madeleine and Max, and my mom Sue. I'd also like to express my appreciation for the sage editorial guidance of Jennika Baines, senior acquisitions editor, and the keen remarks of Judy Barnes, development editor, with the American Psychological Association. You supported me through the process and helped me stay true to the simple mission of helping people feel confident in learning mixed methods. The honest quotes from my interviews and correspondence with Drs. Archibald, Creamer, Levitt, McCrudden, and Nzabonimpa helped bring mixed methods down to earth for the reader and make it feel more human. With the additional feedback from peer reviewers (thank you, whoever you are!), I was able to make my research explanations more exacting. The wonderfully pensive and questioning comments from the advisory board of students and alumni rounded out the editing and improvement cycle. For this, I'd like to thank Drexel dragons Tajma Cameron, Vida Manalang, Leah Sodowick, Jenna Damico, and Onyinyechi Serena Osuagwu and to George Mason doctoral student Megan Stutesman.

HOW TO MIX METHODS

INTRODUCTION

Welcome to *How to Mix Methods: A Guide to Sequential, Convergent, and Experimental Research Designs*! If you are intrigued, curious, or even a little skeptical about how to design a mixed methods research project, then this book is for you. It's also for those teaching a mixed methods class and mentoring others in mixed methods research. *Mixed methods research* is the purposeful design, combination, and integration of at least one qualitative and at least one quantitative research method into a comprehensive research project that incorporates multiple ways of making sense of the social world (Greene, 2007). For many reasons, researchers developed mixed methods when single-method studies alone did not suffice to answer research questions or hypotheses: to explain quantitative results with rich qualitative data, to enhance the cultural validity of measures with new items representing lived experiences garnered from focus groups, or to understand the voices of patients during medical interventions through interviews, for example.

This book can help you if you have experience in qualitative research but not quantitative research, or vice versa, and want to learn how to mix methods. It may also be a great resource if you are working with a team to

https://doi.org/10.1037/0000404-001
How to Mix Methods: A Guide to Sequential, Convergent, and Experimental Research Designs, by J. Katz-Buonincontro

complement and balance your methodological expertise. In addition to standard quantitative and qualitative data, you may be considering the choices you have with unconventional data that you haven't learned about through a class or prior research experience—data that do not include words or numbers, such as photographs, maps, or other types of visual or multimodal data that conjoin sound and movement (e.g., video data). As a result, you may be searching for the best way to combine qualitative and quantitative data to craft a mixed methods design that is feasible within a set context or timeline.

Sometimes, it can be confusing to figure out how to sequence and bring together data that are meaningful without adopting what can be called "the kitchen sink approach" of pulling together different types of data and retrospectively hoping the data make sense. As in my book *How to Interview and Conduct Focus Groups* (Katz-Buonincontro, 2022), I'll walk you through essential steps to avoid some common mistakes and to clarify confusing parts of mixed methods designs.

WHY A NEW MIXED METHODS BOOK?

Several mixed methods books are on the market, and this one is different. In today's world, your time is at a premium, and you may feel you need to learn research methods FAST. I hear you! So, I've written this book using clear and concise steps situated in the core mixed methods literature. The recommended steps are cross-checked against the literature and experts as well as pulled from my teaching and research experience to ensure they are sound. They also reflect the American Psychological Association's mixed methods article reporting standards (MMARS; Levitt et al., 2018) and other standards published in handbooks, books, and journals that presaged the MMARS. As a result, *How to Mix Methods* can help you navigate how to design a sound, rigorous project.

While many mixed methods books and handbooks are excellent, some are long or wordy. Mixed method articles and books take many forms of writing, and some scholarship uses complicated terminology. Older mixed methods articles exempt key steps in methodological integration, mostly because the field did not require it. The nomenclature and descriptions of mixed methods designs can be hard to understand. Sometimes, scholars use complex terms like "mixed methods embedded experimental design." Unpacking this design is like peeling back layers of an onion. The design presumes understanding in (a) experimental research, (b) mixed methods research, and (c) the overlap between the two designs in the placement of qualitative research before, during, or after the experiment. And that's a lot to unpack!

How to Mix Methods can help you break down experimental designs so you can see your choices more clearly and begin a project using simple steps. Once you get a handle on your key design, you may want to complement it with handbooks in specialized mixed methods areas (such as the health fields). As such, this book is not exhaustive or representative of every mixed methods design. Rather, it describes basic mixed methods with essential steps. Individual, highly specialized qualitative and quantitative designs can be referenced in other books. Advanced statistical analyses and qualitative analyses are not explained in detail, as other books address these areas. Multimethod studies that include biological sample collection with quantitative surveys but no qualitative data, for example, are excluded.

SHEDDING FEARS

The word "research" may connote rigor and high standards, causing you to experience a dash of anxiety. To some, research reinforces the idea of academic privilege because researchers need a doctoral degree to conduct research. It's not uncommon for people to feel they are not smart enough to do research and to be troubled by imposter syndrome. That feeling is reinforced in graduate programs that use the language "pass" and "fail" to describe a student's success based on the quality of research theses or dissertations, so it's no wonder people develop fear about doing research. Many are intrigued by the idea of doing a mixed methods project but are scared that they may not be competent in both quantitative and qualitative research methods. Acknowledging and gradually shedding fears about doing research as you become more familiar with the method will plant the seed of appreciation for mixed methods.

BROADENING OUR METHODOLOGICAL FOCUS

If you identify as either a qualitative researcher or a quantitative researcher, then mixing methods will challenge you to broaden your methodological focus. Studying qualitative research holds a stigma in certain circles, as some people describe qualitative research as not real or valid or claim that it relies on cherry-picking. On the other hand, some researchers might think quantitative researchers whip up their stats to answer any question they want, without care to uphold the integrity of the original hypotheses. It's important to cast these stereotypical beliefs aside because each type of research method has its own purpose and history that can be capitalized upon through mixed methods research. Some people might be concerned that mixed methods designs can potentially compromise the quality of either the quantitative or the qualitative component. When carefully designed, though, mixed methods studies do not skimp or use shortcuts for a method; rather, they attempt to properly join two or more methods together in a logical way that addresses the research questions and/or hypotheses.

THE PURPOSE OF THIS BOOK

Is research fun? For some, it is. For many, research can be fun with the aid of mentors and team members and, hopefully, with a practical resource like this book. This book can help you overcome anxiety when facing timeline delays, equipment shortages, study attrition, and other challenges unique to mixed methods, such as the divergence in quantitative and qualitative results. *How to Mix Methods* is designed to help you carry out a high quality, credible mixed methods research project. It explains basic strategies for mixing qualitative and quantitative research methods with confidence to create a clear and comprehensive project in educational, psychological, health, medical, and other social sciences. This book will help you to design your project, conduct, analyze, and integrate data and to write up and publish your mixed methods research.

LET'S GET MIXING!

Have you ever tried to whip up a bowl of pancake batter but were puzzled by the lumps? If you are a novice baker, like me, you may have tried pulverizing the lumps in vain, only to discover that some lumps are not just okay but in fact are necessary to let the pancakes get nice and puffy later in the cooking process. My efforts to please my hungry kids belied my patience. Likewise, the process of mixing methods can be a little like mixing pancake batter: The lumps are a metaphor for the challenges faced when figuring out how to literally mix qualitative and quantitative data.

A mixed methods project first may be a little "lumpy," but through clarifying your design, implementing it with necessary adjustments, and integrating the qualitative and quantitative data, your mixed methods project can result in a strong and compelling research story that helps you answer important research questions as well as get published, extend your field, attract grant funding, and contribute to solving real-world problems. Each person comes to the practice of mixed methods research in a different way. Mixing methods is not taught in high school, undergraduate courses, or in many graduate programs. So, how can you get started? Let's see how the chapters in this book will set you up for success.

OVERVIEW OF THIS BOOK

This book describes the essential steps in designing a sound mixed methods project. The steps in each chapter are intended to guide you but are not carved in stone. Experienced researchers may choose to adapt them according to their personal preferences or use them to guide and mentor postdocs, students, and colleagues.

Each chapter provides explanations of specific mixed methods designs; describes how essential design principles are used; and points to published studies to clarify the sampling, data collection, analysis, and integration choices used within the context of each mixed methods design. Diagrams accompany each mixed methods design as learning aids to clarify the sequencing of methods. At the end of the book, a glossary lists major terms as a reference for the key definitions in mixed methods research. And lastly, I've included clips from correspondence and interviews I conducted with mixed methods experts to give you their fresh perspectives on the leap they made from single-method research to mixed methods research.

Chapter 1 briefly explains the origins of mixed methods, points out the differences from single-method studies and multimethod studies, and unpacks the definition of mixed methods research and its elements. The processes of working with committees, research teams, and community groups are discussed, as are reflexivity, positionality, and ethics.

Chapter 2 outlines 10 essential features of any mixed methods design. If you get confused, feel lost, or decide to change your design when mixing methods, come back to this chapter to help clarify the commonalities across mixed methods designs. Each of the 10 essential features is explained with (a) a definition, (b) a published example, and (c) a design reflection question. The chapters following go deeper into specific designs to help you refine the selection and operationalization of your project.

Chapter 3 explains steps for sequential mixed methods designs. This design is described before convergent (or parallel) designs and other mixed methods designs because sequential designs are generally the most popular mixed methods research designs. Explanatory sequential mixed method designs often include a survey (quantitative) followed by an interview (qualitative). In sequential mixed methods designs, each phase of data collection is completed separately and then the results are analyzed and interpreted together. Exploratory sequential mixed methods designs flip this order of data collection, using interviews or focus groups first as a core approach to developing or altering a survey or instrument. As such, they are especially appropriate for culture-specific, newly researched, and overlooked areas of study.

Chapter 4 explains the essential steps for convergent mixed methods designs (also called concurrent or parallel designs), which include both qualitative and quantitative methods collected separately or in sequence and then analyzed together. This design works well when the researcher has no conceptual reason to sequence a quantitative and qualitative element or has no time to provide two separate phases in the project. The data transformation method is discussed in terms of converting qualitative data sets into quantitative data sets. In this approach, verbal data or transcriptions can be "qualitized," or analyzed thematically (based on emergent themes), and these themes can then be "quantitized" or counted (numerically).

Chapter 5 provides the essential steps for embedding qualitative methods before, during, or after a psychological, educational, behavioral, or medical experiment using an intervention. Most mixed methods research books rarely discuss experimental designs or reference them as a smaller subset and thus do not provide an entire chapter on this design. Interview or focus group data collection before an experiment allows for stakeholders' input and feedback on research questions and the qualities of the intervention before or as it is being designed. Qualitative data can be used to reveal participants' subjective experience during an experiment, such as obtaining spontaneous verbal reactions to stimuli or situations in randomized conditions. After the intervention, collecting qualitative data can give the researcher the opportunity to ensure the intervention is going as described in the grant or research proposal (fidelity of implementation).

Chapter 6 covers mixed methods validity, triangulation, and the integration of quantitative and qualitative results and joint displays. Many books refer to integration briefly or do not clarify the junctures at which integration can occur. Thus, Chapter 6 defines four types of integration: sampling integration, data collection integration, analysis integration, and results integration. A discussion of joint displays, or graphical displays that represent the overlap or divergence of the qualitative and quantitative results, focuses on three types of displays: classic side-by-side tables, color-coded joint displays, and creative joint displays.

Chapter 7 offers strategies for writing up, presenting, publishing, and planning a grant proposal for projects using mixed methods designs. Writing tips focus on whether to keep both quantitative and qualitative components together in a concise manner to meet journal word-length requirements or to separate them. Publication strategies are important because mixed methods research projects include multiple data sets, which can be challenging to report in one succinct manuscript.

Finally, at the end of the book you will find three appendices. Appendix A is an at-a-glance review of the major mixed methods designs described in this book. It is a quick reference for gauging your progress toward completion of your mixed methods project, especially with your team. If you've forgotten how to do a step, you can easily flip back to the right chapter and read the detailed explanation again. Appendix B includes a list of journals that publish mixed methods studies. Appendix C lists programs and professional organizations in mixed methods. In addition, the glossary lists key definitions important in mixed methods research.

By the end of the book, you will be able to

- Identify the 10 essential design elements of all mixed methods research, no matter the specific design

- Clearly distinguish between the purpose of three different core mixed methods designs

- Figure out which design works best for your research, considering adaptations to suit your own unique context, research aims, and the requirements of your program, research team, research partners (e.g., a clinic, school, or teacher), or grant

- Identify and describe appropriate strategies to establish validity and to strengthen your mixed methods design

- Practice ways to integrate the qualitative and quantitative strands of your mixed methods project, including using a joint display

- Determine the complementary skills you may need to shore up through further reading, classes, or collaborations with other researchers

- Develop effective presenting and writing strategies, including developing a publication or grant application plan for your mixed methods research project

Enjoy reading, discussing, and sharing these chapters!

1 DEFINITIONS, ORIGINS, AND PRACTICES OF MIXED METHODS INQUIRY

Let's look more closely at why researchers mix methods, before learning how to mix methods. You might be wondering, how do researchers define mixed methods, and what makes mixed methods research unique and different from single-method studies that are either quantitative or qualitative? Many researchers are drawn to the novelty of combining methods, but it can be

In this chapter, you'll reflect on why mixed methods research suits your research topic and identify what makes mixed methods studies different from single-method or multimethod studies. You'll review the distinctive features of qualitative and quantitative research methods and mixed methods inquiry. Reflexivity and positionality are defined and then discussed as ways to harbor your passion for research while extending the passion to research with communities and with mixed methods research teams. Taken together, these critical skills will prepare you for diving deeper into 10 essential design principles in Chapter 2.

https://doi.org/10.1037/0000404-002
How to Mix Methods: A Guide to Sequential, Convergent, and Experimental Research Designs, by J. Katz-Buonincontro

challenging to mix methods, especially while learning the basics of quantitative and qualitative research. As we dig deeper into mixed methods, we will consider the idea of comprehensiveness so that your project adequately straddles and integrates both qualitative and quantitative methods. Attention to comprehensiveness helps prevent the "frankenproject" (as in Frankenstein) from appearing disjointed.

DEFINITIONS

Mixed methods research is the purposeful design, combination, and integration of at least one qualitative and at least one quantitative research method into a comprehensive research project that incorporates multiple ways of making sense of the social world (Greene, 2007). Later in this chapter, I explain how mixed methods research evolved parallel to multimethod research but has matured to include both qualitative and quantitative data (and other types of data such as drawings or geotagged coordinates).

The emphasis on combination is based on the concept of triangulation of data developed by Jick (1979). The more recent concept of integration derives from mixed methods scholars Creamer (2018) and Creswell and Plano Clark (2018). The multifaceted philosophical view of the social world grounded in data is an important criterion that derives from longstanding work of scholar Rachel Greene (2007), who helped pioneer mixed methods in the field of evaluation and thus popularized its use. In this book, I also focus on the idea of comprehensiveness because it's common to struggle with writing up the totality of the project once data have been collected and analyzed. To learn mixed methods, qualitative and quantitative research definitions are important. This book assumes you know the details of basic research inquiry, including how to define the scope of a research problem and to search methodically for related prior studies in a given area. Following is a refresher of key terms.

Quantitative research methods focus on the "what" in a mixed methods project. Quantitative research investigates human behavior by posing research questions and hypotheses. These hypotheses are tested by collecting quantitative data, or numerical scores based on responses to a survey, instrument, or test. In quantitative research, hypotheses are statements that explain the predicted relationships between variables. The relationships among the quantitative data are then tested statistically. These tests form the basis of predictions and generalizations. Mixed methods have historically privileged quantitative research, but there is an increasing effort to balance out the representation of both methods or to explicitly emphasize either qualitative or quantitative methods during the design phase at the outset of a project.

Qualitative research methods elucidate the "what" in terms of identifying important thoughts, beliefs, and experiences. But qualitative research methods also focus on the experiential, relational, social, and historical contexts—or time-related phases—of these thoughts in terms of "why" and "how" a person thinks, acts, or experiences a situation. With open-ended research questions, researchers using qualitative methods aim to understand how and why people think, feel, act, and behave through word-based (as opposed to numerical) data. Interview responses, focus group responses, observations, journals, and field memos are examples of qualitative data.

Some mixed methods projects use exploratory qualitative research questions at the beginning of a quantitative project or an explanatory qualitative research question in the second phase of the project. It can be misleading to limit the potential of qualitative methods this way, as qualitative research questions may provide the impetus for a mixed methods project. Transferability is a principle used to infer from qualitative results, as opposed to prediction and generalizability used in quantitative research. Mixed methods research can be suitable for addressing many different psychological, social, behavioral, educational, medical, and health research issues when quantitative or qualitative research alone tells only part of the story.

USING QUANTITATIVE METHODS WITH QUALITATIVE METHODS TO TACKLE INCOMPLETE UNDERSTANDINGS

Qualitative-only or a quantitative-only projects may be simpler to conduct, but they sometimes leave a slightly hollow feeling afterwards. Single-method projects cause us to wonder why and how the data make sense. An example research question might be, "How do we understand complex behaviors, such as intimate partner violence, that can't be investigated through experimental designs?" Some researchers have questions about why people rate themselves a certain way, why certain variables relate to each other in the way they do, or how surveys can be better crafted to capture people's lived realities.

Other single-method investigations might examine whether measurement tools are truly responsive to humanity and sensitive to the inherent diversity in our society. Some researchers are interested in developing good ways to study elusive, fleeting, or complicated dimensions of the human experience. These Big Questions, with capital "B" and "Q," suggest the possibility of more than one research question that could lend themselves well to mixed methods inquiry.

Although we may never be able to completely answer these Big Questions, it's important as researchers to open our minds to a full range of investigatory techniques with small "q" questions that lend themselves nicely to mixed methods, such as

> How does students' described experience (interviews or focus groups; qualitative) correspond to their classroom behavior (observations, either qualitative or quantitative, depending on the methodological approach), their self-rated experience (Survey 1; quantitative) and teacher ratings of their academic performance (Survey 2; quantitative)?

Of course, this question can be broken down into individual subquestions: How do students rate their own creativity, and what is the factor structure of the creativity scales? (quantitative) and how do students describe their experience being creative while learning engineering design? (qualitative). If these research questions were addressed by independent studies, the data are unlikely to suggest a very complete picture of student learning.

It's possible to extend this example mixed methods inquiry even further. For instance, we may also consider additional forms of data such as arts-based data or photographs: How do students' self-portraits, either those drawn by hand or selfies (photographs), elaborate on the themes represented in the interviews and the student ratings collected via surveys?

Taken together, we can see that the qualitative data represents narrative experience, the quantitative data represents numeric ratings, and the visual data represents self-referential symbols, colors, and shapes that convey certain themes. Each set of data might be sufficient by itself, but when data are considered together, we can see that they might shed light on a specific phenomenon, such as student learning experience, in a holistic manner.

Research questions are like an archipelago, or little islands. Our task as mixed methods researchers is to connect the islands with bridges. By placing individual questions side by side in one mixed methods study, we can start to see potential connections across them while preserving the integrity of each separate question.

Based on the notion of holistic mixed methods inquiry, here are four reasons why researchers mix methods.

Learning New Methods

Many researchers like to stretch their methodological skill sets by learning new aspects about methods. Combining methods can provide great satisfaction in developing one's methodological chops. When we work collaboratively with team members with mutual interest and accountability, mixed methods research projects help push us to use open and transparent science to examine real problems. In my experience as a methods instructor, researcher, student supervisor, grant writer, and associate dean of research, I've observed that mixed methods research holds an intuitive and widespread appeal to students and researchers. It requires an understanding at least rooted firmly in either qualitative or quantitative research but with a deep appreciation for both.

Making Social and Scientific Progress

Many people want concrete results from research to spark real-world change (a review of the related philosophy of science called "pragmatism" appears later in this chapter). This orientation speaks to our humanity and our desire as researchers to connect with other people to make the world better through research. Advancing a field is rewarding and holds the prospect of addressing limitations, gaps, or deficiencies in a specific research area. For example, researchers might want to explore why or how people think a certain way and what kinds of experiences they have, but the prevailing survey or instrument has been normed with a White population. As human science and specifically psychological science is Eurocentric and based mostly on WEIRD (Western, educated, industrialized, rich, democratic) samples using college students (see Aiello et al., 2021), researchers and funders are increasingly concerned with diversifying study samples to represent world populations accurately (Gurven, 2018). This work aims to broaden psychology to make it more inclusive of those who identify as Black, Indigenous, or people of color (BIPOC; Aiello et al., 2021). Such work could call for a mixed methods approach to modify or revise surveys and instruments according to a culture-specific group or groups. For example, a researcher using a sequential exploratory mixed methods design might first conduct focus groups to build a new instrument or to adapt an existing one, pilot it, and use it with a diverse group of participants. As such, many mixed methods researchers don't see advancing the field at the expense of benefiting society: They hope to use their research in applied ways to make social, educational, or clinical progress in addition to scientific progress.

Amplifying Research Creativity

In addition to helping people by making scientific and social progress, mixed methods research calls forth our inner creative ilk for exploring data in ways that do not jeopardize the integrity but enhance the meaning. Mixed methods projects require innovative graphical displays, called joint displays, that conjoin the results of both qualitative and quantitative data. Joint displays reinforce learning about a research problem from different angles and seeing reality in many ways. Not only does mixed methods research speak to researcher creativity, but it also speaks to capturing human creativity more accurately. As implied in the sample set of research questions presented earlier in the chapter, mixed methods research can include art, video, maps, and various other examples of human creativity and expression. Research methods are always growing, changing, and trending. It's impossible to be omniscient when it comes to research methods because people are constantly expressing themselves in new ways and in new contexts, especially with social media and the further expansion of artificial intelligence. Doing mixed methods research almost guarantees being creative with data representation and representation of human communication and artistry.

Spanning Boundaries

A final reason for mixing methods is to span boundaries across fields and across schools of training in one method. Mixed methods projects reach an audience conceivably wider than just a qualitative or just a quantitative research audience. In the past, university research cultures reinforced affiliation with either a qualitative or quantitative "camp," or school of thought, and with the various social groups within these camps. Now, many students and researchers are interested in bridging these divides and working across groups. As a result, many researchers care about communicating their research to a wide audience, which can be helped by using mixed methods. Later in this chapter, I discuss how mixed methods researchers actively collaborate and value team research. Some teams are multidisciplinary, including members from psychology, medicine, education, and/or engineering. In sum, mixed methods research spans methodological boundaries, people boundaries, and disciplinary boundaries.

CURRENT TRENDS

The mixed methods research field is at the cutting edge of emergent methods, meaning that scholars are developing a new vocabulary, and interpreting these terms can require effort. For this reason, in this book I take the just-right "Goldilocks approach": I aim to strike a balance between simplicity and comprehensiveness to explain mixed methods design strategies in plain language. For all these reasons, and many more, designing mixed methods studies can be gratifying and can hold a potentially high payoff. Let's look more closely at mixed methods origins.

Mixed Methods Origins

Mixed methodology continues to develop within the context of the ongoing quest for perfecting research methods, understanding truth in science, and debating intersubjectivity (how people come to arrive at a truth or multiple truths; Bourdieu & Wacquant, 1992). Depending on your field, mixed methods research might be common. But perhaps the researchers you know don't conduct mixed methods research or teach it in your program or college. You might be wondering, how did the field start? Mixed methods research has roots in the early 1970s as part of a larger movement to explore the meaning of rigor and threats to validity, or accuracy, in specific research methods. Researchers were also growing weary of the so-called paradigm wars that narrowly constrained social science methods and focused on issues such as internal validity (accuracy of measurement) with little attention to ecological, face, and cultural validity (how the context, people, and cultural values shape research).

The paradigm wars led to the development of the scientific interest in pragmatism (Tashakkori & Teddlie, 1998) and the concept of triangulation, or comparing multiple data sets (Jick, 1979). Mixed methods research grew into a legitimate field in the late 1980s (Brewer & Hunter, 2006) and early 1990s as a novel approach to program evaluation (e.g., Greene et al., 1989) and case study (e.g., Patton, 2002). With new books, scholars such as Creswell (1995) and Tashakkori and Teddlie (1998) consolidated the various approaches to combining quantitative and qualitative methods to promote an understanding of mixed methods. The methodology then branched out in the 2000s, spanning many designs while also exploring how to uphold standards of validity and reliability in the social sciences.

The scientific philosophy of using many methods to study one phenomenon dates back centuries to philosophers such as Whewell (1840), who put forth the concept of consilience (Brewer & Hunter, 2006). Consilience is the scientific effort to examine a problem with multiple independent measures. It implies that the measures should converge, a concern that mostly pertains to multimethods. However, this approach is not used as a standard in the area of mixed methods, where the term "triangulation" is used frequently (Jick, 1979) to mean comparing multiple data sources, including qualitative ones. In mixed methods inquiry, researchers explore how qualitative and quantitative results relate to one another and do not necessarily assume that qualitative results should confirm quantitative results. Though researchers use quantitative and qualitative methods to examine a similar construct in a mixed methods study, they are not attempting to replicate measurement or converge on a single truth. Therefore, differences across quantitative and qualitative methods are often found in mixed methods and used as a rich source for expanding understandings of the data.

At their core, multimethod studies pursue multideterminism (Schmitt, 2006). This concept is a scientific principle for investigating various antecedents, causes, and reasons to explain an observed behavior using a multimethod research inquiry. Multideterminism could also be extended to mixed methods with the caveat that it would need to be expanded to include qualitative aims that extend beyond causes and to explain additional phenomena such as interpersonal relationships, social contexts, lived experiences, and individual perspectives.

Mixed methods research designs differ from multimethod designs in several important ways. Multimethod measurement design developed in psychology (see Brewer & Hunter, 2006). The multitrait multimethod matrix (MTMM) developed by Campbell and Fiske (1959) helped researchers distinguish between convergent validity (evidence confirming same results) and discriminant validity (variance attributable to method). Essentially, MTMM examines several separate quantitative operational definitions of one construct. For instance, an MTMM study could use a physiological stress measure combined with behavioral observation of stress. MTMM helped set the stage for further research using multiple methods together in one study for the purposes of multiple operationalism (Campbell & Fiske, 1959).

Later, MTMM expanded to include qualitative research methods as an important strand of a research project (Onwuegbuzie et al., 2010). Multimethod studies may use multiple qualitative strands, multiple quantitative strands, or both. However, the strands coexist but do not necessarily mix or integrate (Anguera et al., 2018; see Table 1.1). In addition, incorporating data from arts-based research is now recognized as legitimate in mixed methods research (Archibald, 2016).

Historically, many mixed methods designs have emphasized quantitative data, in part because more quantitative researchers than qualitative researchers were using designs identified as multimethod research. In the early 2000s, a research movement to reify experimental educational research as the gold standard relegated qualitative research to a somewhat inferior status (Creswell et al., 2006). Since then, qualitative and mixed methods

TABLE 1.1. Comparison of Multimethod and Mixed Methods Research

Dimension	Multimethod	Mixed methods
Scientific philosophy	Multideterminism	Balancing positivism with constructivism and interpretivism with pragmatism
Quantitative data	Coexisting (not purposefully mixed)	Integrated with qualitative data
Qualitative data	Coexisting (not purposefully mixed)	Integrated with quantitative data
Secondary data/ arts-based data	Not used in multimethod research	Integrated with qualitative and quantitative data

Note. Positivism is a theory of logic underlying quantitative research that requires objective scientific evidence relying on statistics, whereas constructivism centers on the importance of subjective knowledge and experiences as part of constructing reality, which is foundational to qualitative research. Interpretivism focuses on the multiplicity of reality, and pragmatism emphasizes the applied practice of research.

researchers have repositioned qualitative research at the heart of mixed methods or even as a dominant method in a mixed methods study. As a result of continued debate and clarification about the proper aims of different research methods and their appropriate use, it is now common practice to articulate whether either quantitative or qualitative strands are prioritized. Oftentimes, mixed methods researchers explicitly state which method has priority status or even that they have equal status. In sum, it's now more common for mixed methods designs to incorporate a collection of qualitative data as an essential feature of the mixed methods design, such as grounded theory mixed methods (Creamer, 2022).

Mixed methods research has become more acceptable in fields that include self-report data, qualitative interviews, and focus groups. Focus groups and interviews have gained acceptance because of their capacity to engage communities, include marginalized voices, and expand representation. As such, mixed methods first developed a toehold in fields in which human voice in the research process was more considerable, such as education, the health sciences, and community and cultural psychology. Now, students and researchers in psychology and the social sciences increasingly foray into the world of designing mixed methods research within the established frameworks of experiments, program and grant evaluation, social justice studies, case studies, and arts-based and arts therapy research.

Multiple Truth Orientation

Valuing multiple truths means casting a wide philosophical net to value multiple aspects of the social world. It extends Schmitt's (2006) emphasis on multideterminism in multimethod research by valuing qualitative data in addition to quantitative data. The social world could pertain to any number or type of lived experiences or developmental processes, including schooling, growing up, being incarcerated, living with a disease/medical condition, or a combination therein. A multiple truth orientation builds on mixed methods program evaluator Greene's (2007) philosophical orientation of seeing social worlds from multiple viewpoints. Holding multiple if not competing truths or viewpoints about social realities is core to building a mixed methods philosophical orientation. The concept of multiple truth orientation also relates to intersectionality, which is a psychological theory positing that a person's intersecting identities, such as race, gender, and sexuality, differently shape experiences and behaviors (Huynh & Farhadi Langroudi, 2016). Mixed methods research can incorporate the study of intersectionality by representing identity with both quantitative indicators and qualitative descriptors, for example.

A multiple truth orientation takes good teamwork. Successful mixed methods teams extend beyond a qualitative and a quantitative researcher working together on separate parts of the project. Contemporary mixed methods researchers form a balanced appreciation for both strands of research. How do teams do this when they are trained principally in either qualitative or quantitative research? Ideally, teams conceptualize the mixed methods design, study purpose, and rationale together before data are collected. During this phase of research design, the team discusses the perceived benefits of various designs, suspends judgment about the efficacy of a method, explores the pros and cons of each method, and then decides on a mixed methods design that can be adjusted when necessary.

Pragmatism

Pragmatism has a strong foundation in psychology and education that is core to mixed methods inquiry. It's a philosophy of science derived from the Greek word for "deed" and the Latin word for "to do," "to make," or "to create." This strand of philosophy focuses on purposeful human activity (Allmark & Machaczek, 2018). The field of pragmatism stems from a late 19th-century movement to center philosophy, research, and science on the investigation of practical applications, such as how beliefs shape action (see Dewey, 1967; James, 1981; Peirce, 1932–1958).

Though the field was formed more than a century ago, mixed methods researchers reinvigorated the principles of pragmatism for the purpose of conducting mixed methods. As mentioned earlier in the chapter, part of the appeal of pragmatism as a guiding philosophy is the practical and optimistic focus on promoting social progress, which relates to valuing multiple truths and even honoring people's intersectional identities, for example. Importantly, pragmatism places the guiding inquiry at the center of mixed methods research (Tebes, 2012). That means either quantitative or qualitative research can be used and sequenced, depending on the nature of the question. Pragmatism bypasses the issue of getting stuck in seeing research in only one way and reflects the importance of community discourse regarding the purpose of research (Bernstein, 1988). For years, psychologists, philosophers, and scientists have debated the scientific value of phenomenology (subjective, firsthand lived experience) and behaviorism (describing, predicting, and characterizing observable and measurable behavior). Rogers (1964) referred to those in staunch camps as essentialist thinkers who reject other ways of doing science.

Holding a multiple truth orientation allows for a way to celebrate the contributions of various scientific approaches, tensions notwithstanding. Pragmatism straddles a constructivist view (socially constructed, subjective realities) characteristic of much qualitative research and a positivist view (of a single objective reality), the major paradigm of quantitative research. Going back and forth between deduction (examining data) and induction (inferences based on the data) is called abduction (Morgan, 2007). One example of abduction in a mixed methods study is examining participants' unexpected comments added to survey responses (Feilzer, 2010). Instead of ignoring these comments, Feilzer used them in a pragmatic way to enrich and deepen the data analysis. In a stand-alone quantitative study, the comments might be categorized as unnecessary; in a qualitative-only study, the comments might be deemed insufficient for data collection and analysis. Treated comprehensively in tandem, Feilzer was able to bridge these two data sets.

Other researchers advocate for use of mixed methods to better understand pragmatic issues like posttreatment processes to advance psychoanalytic science, which has historically undervalued narrative stories about treatment experience (Tillman et al., 2011). Researchers have adopted mixed methods to ground their fields more squarely in pragmatic issues, such as exploring the multidimensionality of health services focused on patients in speech and language therapy (Glogowska, 2011), understanding jurors' impressions of attorneys to advance criminology (Trahan & Stewart, 2013), and describing patients' experiences of illness in addition to their cognitive coping strategies to advance the field of health psychology (Bishop, 2015).

BUILDING MIXED METHODS RESEARCH TEAMS

In addition to the technical compatibility of research methods, professional and interpersonal compatibility are important guiding principles for forming a strong team to conduct mixed methods research. In contrast to single-study research projects, mixed methods teams often include researchers with different types of methodological expertise as well as liaisons, collaborators, research partners in various communities, and key professionals of practice such as teachers, translators, and clinicians. Good mixed methods teams generally produce good research and scholarship.

Research teams form in different ways, for different reasons. Mixed methods projects can include people who have never worked together before and have different sets of training. Or mixed methods teams might be natural outgrowths of existing collaborations. Researchers might need to seek complementary expertise to round out the team's strengths for a new project or grant application.

How does a researcher form, lead, and participate on a mixed methods team? Generally, the "leader" is the principal investigator or researcher who instigates and forms the project and who organizes and pulls the team through delays, unanticipated issues, or disorganization. If you are the leader, once you've considered who should be on your team and confirmed their interest, think about how to form the team identity. The following are some helpful team-building strategies. If you are a participant on the team but not the official leader, your input is just as valuable; these tips will help you, too.

- **Share the story of how you started your research.** People are drawn together around a passion to solve a problem or to explore burning questions through mixed methods research. To initiate a discussion, bring or photocopy this first chapter with the section on the four reasons people are drawn to mixed methods and the definition highlighted.

  - Team-building prompts: What is your research area, and what excites you about working on this team project? Which reason(s) for doing mixed methods research resonate with you: learning new methods, making social and scientific progress, amplifying research creativity, and/or spanning boundaries? What strengths and special concerns do you bring to the table?

- **Codraft team agreements that explicate your values.** Let people explore what matters to them and then look for commonalities across the values. Use the principles of openness and transparency to share, store, collect, and work on documents collaboratively. Even though your team might gel well, unexpected situations that sometimes pop up can be navigated better when the team is built on a foundation of shared understanding and trust.

  – Team-building prompts: What are your values? How would you characterize your communication style? Does your institution have any regulations about sharing data, and what are the best ways to do so?

• **Talk about your leadership style.** Take the guesswork out of collaboration. Try to be direct but calm when you communicate. Reinforce people positively with each interaction. Think about the power conferred upon you as a result of institutional or organizational status. Contemplate ways to balance power differentials across team members. Talk about taking advantage of the unique resources across all team members. Give each person an opportunity to lead a small part of the project and team meetings, thus differentiating people's roles on the team.

  – Team-building prompts: How do you learn best, and how would you characterize your preferences for working in groups? What's an area of the project you'd like to lead?

• **Design a symbol for the team and a simple project calendar.** Visual symbols are a touchstone for people to create unity, build their team identity, and remember their goals. If you have time, maybe you can invent a new symbol and/or an acronym that combines the strengths of the research team. With multiple projects that compete for everyone's attention, you can indicate key milestones with a Gantt chart, for example, that shows the chronological steps to the project in a horizontal table. Strive to be flexible and compassionate about changes in deadlines and deliverables to accommodate the shifting research landscape, study attrition, and other things not easy to control.

  – Team-building prompts: What's a good acronym for our team project that's easy to remember? What's a visual symbol that reflects the acronym and represents our work to the public?

• **Foster teamwork.** Investigator triangulation is a potential benefit of mixed methods teams, but not unless it's deliberately fostered. It includes looking at the research question from different perspectives (Archibald, 2016). Encourage students and younger researchers to take a stab at developing new skills, such as drafting an interview protocol or designing a research poster. Determine if you need to work with people in communities other than or in addition to your own organization or institution, and explore a mechanism for establishing a liaison and partner.

- – Team-building prompts: What skills do we need on our team? What's missing, and how can we shore up our skills in certain areas? What partners would take our project to the next level?

- **Write a positionality statement together.** A positionality statement, or research stance, situates the research team's orientation to the research topic and toward the research collaboration with community research partners and study participants. It might come easy for seasoned researchers or those who have studied education, cultural psychology, sociology, or anthropology and have an awareness of their privilege as academic researchers, but it can also be challenging. You can start a draft of a statement and ask others to add in their reflections on their identity. If you like, you can use the theory of intersectionality to point out how we each hold multiple identities. You may find that team members feel honored to discuss themselves and that they see overlaps across them and discover new facets of their own identities and other team members' identities.

- – Team-building prompts: How might the research project be affected by our identities and expectations? What do we need to be aware of as we navigate the stages of the project?

REFLEXIVITY, BENDING BACK, AND POSITIONALITY

Like wiping down a foggy mirror to try to see the reflection clearly, researchers also try to clarify the purpose for doing research through a process called reflexivity. Reflexivity generally means "ability to bend back." In this context, reflexivity highlights how researchers reflect on engagement in every phase of the research process (Bourdieu & Wacquant, 1992). Reflexivity is core to social science research and is mostly used in qualitative research, not as much in quantitative research. Nevertheless, it's becoming key to mixed methods research. The reason qualitative researchers value reflexivity and awareness of their research impact is that they work with people in ways that might be personal so they may gain insight to perspectives, beliefs, stories, and personal reflections. Practicing reflexivity includes stating how researchers' backgrounds influence the research (Levitt et al., 2018).

Taking reflexivity seriously, mixed methods researchers also think about their positionality. Positionality refers to the recognition that knowledge is rooted in a position and is situational (Haraway, 1988). For example, feminist researchers have developed a practice of describing their research standpoints to elucidate how assumptions, values, and biases mold or potentially affect research methods (Hesse-Biber, 2010). Dr. Heidi Levitt, a professor in the Clinical Psychology program within the Department of Psychology at the University of Massachusetts and who helped write the APA mixed methods article reporting standards (Levitt, 2020), explained positionality in this way:

> Considering my positionality means that I don't only consider my expectations as I started out on my research project, but that I consider how my identities and social positions might influence my understanding of the topic that I am studying. This process helps me to be more cognizant of aspects that I might miss and to think about how to adapt my methods so that I am more likely to develop a comprehensive set of findings that apply to a broad range of people within the scope of my question. When I am writing about my positionality, I think carefully about the specific nature and characteristics of the issue I am studying and how it plays out within social and interpersonal systems. This helps me to notice how my own experiences might be limiting and to develop a plan for that specific study to ask questions, invite coauthors, use participatory methods and/or recruit participants who can deepen the understanding produced. (H. Levitt, personal communication, March 6, 2023)

At its essence, writing is a social act that has ethical dimensions. Researchers embracing reflexivity and positionality are respectful about how they write about and portray participants. The act of labeling determines how people are represented, especially when people are stereotyped, misrepresented, or discriminated against in the larger society (e.g., reference to "Arabs as violent terrorists"; Karam et al., 2020).

Mixed methods researchers increasingly include a statement of positionality in research projects to ensure fair representation of participants. Not all mixed methods research articles include a positionality statement, but it's a growing practice. These statements help assure the reader that ethical steps have been taken to develop a supportive and healthy relationship between the researcher and the study participants, one that promotes respectful boundaries and thus mitigates the potential perpetuation of harm when working with community participants. Exhibit 1.1 provides two positionality statements showing how the researchers declared their epistemological stance and navigated power dynamics with informants in mixed methods studies.

PRACTICING OPEN SCIENCE AND REPLICATION

Along with constructing research stances or positionality statements, it is now common to register research questions and hypotheses before collecting and analyzing data. This process is known as preregistration. The purpose

EXHIBIT 1.1. Two Positionality Statements

Mixed Methods Positionality Statement (1)

A researcher's personal experiences and inquiry worldview both play an important role in the research process. I am a critical race educational psychologist whose program of research has been influenced by racialized experiences and a Critical Race Theory inquiry worldview, a worldview dedicated to examining issues of race, racism, and systems of power. In other words, I am not only interested in highlighting and eradicating racial injustices through my research regarding the experiences of African Americans in education, I am also committed to helping expand the manner in which race is examined in the field of educational psychology, including through the discussion of research methodology (DeCuir-Gunby & Schutz, 2014, 2017).

Mixed Methods Positionality Statement (2)

A dimension of positionality that is particularly important in mixed methods research is power relations between the researcher and the researched (Cormode & Hughes, 1999). As data are often collected from different groups of respondents, the mixed methods researcher needs to adapt quickly to changing power relations and this can be challenging. *This was the situation in which I found myself. I tried to maintain equal power relations with all the respondents that cut across top state officials and local farmers.* Yet in practice, some of the top state officials saw me as too young to be asking questions about the government's financial practices and transparency in forest resource management. Some top officials also felt a student should not have been asking some of the questions I was asking. For instance, one stated, "I don't think a student needs this information you are asking for" (Gidi, Forest Manager, February 28, 2006).

On the other hand, some respondents, mainly street-level bureaucrats and local people, perceived me as a privileged Ghanaian because of my level of education and affiliation to a U.K. university. Thus, as my research involved interviewing both elite and ordinary people, my power relations with these respondents changed from one context to the other.

Note. Statement 1 is from "Using Critical Race Mixed Methodology to Explore the Experiences of African Americans in Education," by J. T. DeCuir-Gunby, 2020, *Educational Psychologist, 55*(4), p. 246 (https://doi.org/10.1080/00461520.2020.1793762). Statement 2 is from "Benefits, Challenges, and Dynamism of Positionalities Associated With Mixed Methods Research in Developing Countries: Evidence From Ghana," by J. K. Teye, 2012, *Journal of Mixed Methods Research, 6*(4), p. 388 (https://doi.org/10.1177/1558689812453332).

of preregistration is to prevent false representation of results and to foster a climate of open science. Supplemental materials and data repositories can be noted in an article. As a result, readers can find and access relevant information pertaining to the data and analysis contained in an article. These notations illustrate the principle of open science.

With respect to experimental mixed methods, researchers can conduct replications of studies to clarify the relationships among variables and to extend an experiment with a new condition or adapt the experiment to a new setting and field. The replication can address advancements in science since the original experiment and may extend new theoretical ideas. For example, emerging research might suggest a new approach to studying an enduring idea through replication. If you are replicating a study, cite and summarize that study and explain why a replication is necessary. As the conditions, materials, and/or setting may not be precisely identical to the original study, explain how they are similar.

SUMMARY

This chapter provided guideposts for starting a mixed methods project. I discussed the definition of mixed methods and how it differs from multimethod and single-method studies, and I explained core reasons people get interested in mixed methods research. Multiple truth orientation and pragmatism distinguish mixed methods designs. Positionality was also defined, with some example statements; it is increasingly used but not required in a mixed methods project. I reviewed ways to bridge a quantitative mode of inquiry with a qualitative mode of inquiry to make mixed methods inquiry. Six principles of team building help guide you to embark on the design. So, are you ready to get started with your mixed methods research project? Let's delve into mixed methods research essentials in Chapter 2.

2 MIXED METHODS DESIGN ESSENTIALS

If you feel like you are facing an oncoming storm—a "wintry mix," if you will—of options, possibilities, and questions when designing a mixed methods project, you are not alone! With the right kind of preparation, not only can you ride out the storm, but you can face the eye of the storm with clarity. In this chapter, 10 mixed methods design essentials are presented to help you sort out the onslaught of questions that may be popping into your mind. Each design essential is briefly explained and coupled with one or more examples from published journal articles and simple reflection questions. See Table 2.1 for a quick reference checklist.

One of your first questions might be about what makes a strong mixed methods project, compared to a single-method project, no matter the type of design. Look no further! Chapter 2 is a good place to turn if you want to get familiar with the essentials of designing a mixed methods project and find yourself short on time. I explain why these design essentials are important based on the latest trends in the field and the mixed methods article reporting standards (MMARS; Levitt et al., 2018).

https://doi.org/10.1037/0000404-003
How to Mix Methods: A Guide to Sequential, Convergent, and Experimental Research Designs, by J. Katz-Buonincontro

TABLE 2.1. Ten Mixed Methods Design Essentials

Essential design element for a mixed methods project	Reflection questions
1. A persuasive research problem	What are the larger societal, psychological, educational, or medical problems that make this research exigent, timely, and relevant?
	What extant data from an authorized database, dashboard, survey, census, or other measure can further elucidate the research problem?
2. An intentional mixed methods rationale	What is the rationale for using mixed methods as opposed to a multimethod or a single-method (quantitative or qualitative) research design?
	How does using mixed methods pioneer or break new ground in a specific research area?
3. Dual study aims	What is the simplest, most direct way to state the aims of the mixed methods project, relating back to solving the research problem?
	What are the quantitative aims (e.g., to measure change) and the qualitative aims (e.g., to understand experience), and how are they balanced?
4. Stated gaps in single-study research and in the literature	How do the methodological gaps in single-method studies inform my mixed methods design?
	What are the key results, perceived affordances, and drawbacks of the methods used in prior studies (mixed methods, quantitative, or qualitative)?
	What exemplar studies employ the particular mixed methods design I'm using?
5. A theory-anchored study	What anchor theory guides both selecting quantitative measures and crafting the qualitative protocols?
	Looking forward, how do I anticipate the study results will contribute to the original theory that I cite in the literature review?
	How might theory anchor the mixed methods project to develop a new model for applied practice?
6. A combination of research questions, hypotheses, and/or mixed methods research questions	What is my basic, broad research question?
	How will I break down the basic research question into qualitative and quantitative research questions or hypotheses?
	For the quantitative data, is a hypothesis more suitable than a research question?
	What mixed methods research question integrates both the qualitative and quantitative research question(s)?

TABLE 2.1. Ten Mixed Methods Design Essentials (*Continued*)

Essential design element for a mixed methods project	Reflection questions
7. One or two sampling stages	What is my sampling strategy for the first strand, phase, or wave of data in my mixed methods project?
	Do I use the same sampling strategy to collect the second strand of data, or do I need to construct a secondary (smaller), subsample from the primary sample?
8. A mixed methods diagram	Would I start the diagram with either a qualitative or quantitative strand, or both?
	What quantitative data do I want to "explain" with qualitative data (if any)?
	What qualitative phenomenon do I want to "explore" to then shape the quantitative phase (if any)?
	Which symbols (e.g., squares, circles, ovals) in the diagram represent the study phases in a clear manner?
9. Ethical collaborations with research site and participants	What is the process for submitting the human subjects protocol?
	If working with community partner(s), is there a separate organizational review process for granting permission to conduct research in addition to the university institutional review board?
	How will I collect and describe participant demographic and background data?
	Do I need to conduct a power analysis to determine the number of participants for the sample in the quantitative strand?
	What are the best ways to recruit and enroll participants in the study?
10. A comprehensive description of the quantitative measure(s) and qualitative data protocol(s)	How does the data collection tie back to the research questions and type of mixed methods design?
	Which quantitative measures best represent the quantitative strand?
	Which qualitative data protocols best represent the qualitative strand?

Note. These design essentials are not locked steps, so you may approach them in an order that best suits your project and team.

The order of design essentials is not locked in. There's no one absolute way to start research. For example, you might start based on your team, supervisor, work schedule, grant funding cycle, or the aspirations of your lab, school, clinic, or community research partner. You can always circle back to these design essentials as you conceptualize your project.

> The 10 mixed methods design essentials in this chapter will help ground you so that you can stay focused on designing a quality, rigorous project in the face of complexity when seeking to combine two or more distinct quantitative and qualitative methodological phases. A published example of each feature illustrates one way to effectively address that design essential. The reflection question(s) are designed to stimulate ideas and ways you can adapt each design essential to your own study.

DESIGN ESSENTIAL 1: A PERSUASIVE RESEARCH PROBLEM

Describing the research problem helps situate your mixed methods research project in a societal, psychological, educational, or medical context. That's why it's important to reference carefully selected statistics and/or research reports. This information can show how the research problem is relevant, timely, and exigent. As a result, your mixed methods project will likely command the reader's attention. You can show historical trends or current statistical information about the prevalence of a problem or issue within or across local, regional, national, or international communities. Including statistics that characterize the nature and scope of your research topic can establish the legitimacy of a problem in the public's eye. For example, researchers examining the effects of COVID-19 on schools in the United States could use publicly available data from national surveys run by the Institute of Education Sciences (e.g., https://ies.ed.gov/schoolsurvey/).

Depending on the nature of the research problem, data dashboards can be valuable for writing up a persuasive research problem. For instance, a mixed methods project examining health disparities could use the U.S. National Institutes of Health's data dashboard (U.S. National Institutes of Health, 2022). Additionally, policy think tanks and research institutes offer research-based reports and briefs that can be cited. For example, the RAND Corporation (https://www.rand.org/) publishes online reports on public policy issues such as homeland security, opioid addiction, and disaster research, and The Brookings Institute (https://www.brookings.

edu/programs/) outlines politics, government, military, and foreign affairs issues. The *Congressional Quarterly Magazine* (https://us.sagepub.com/en-us/nam/cq-magazine), the Pew Research Center (https://www.pewresearch.org/), and other independent foundations also provide summaries of trends in topical areas.

Published Example

In the introduction to their mixed methods study, Rashid and Iguchi (2019) used data from the 2013 UNICEF report *Female Genital Mutilation/Cutting: A Statistical Overview and Exploration of the Dynamics of Change* to characterize the prevalence of the human rights violation of female genital cutting (FGC) practices in African countries, particularly in Egypt:

> In 2013, UNICEF reported that an estimated 125 million girls and women have been cut in 29 countries in Africa and the Middle East and 30 million more are at risk of being cut in the coming decade. In 2012, the United Nations (UN) general assembly adopted a resolution to intensify global efforts to eliminate FGC. (p. 1)

Reflection Questions

When describing a persuasive research problem, ask yourself the following questions:

- What are the larger societal, psychological, educational, or medical problems that make this research exigent (i.e., pressing), timely, and relevant?

- What extant data from an authorized database, dashboard, or survey can further elucidate the research problem?

DESIGN ESSENTIAL 2: AN INTENTIONAL MIXED METHODS RATIONALE

One of the most recent rhetorical trends in designing a mixed methods research project is to provide a rationale for using mixed methods designs after the research problem is described. According to MMARS (Levitt, 2020), it's important to provide an aims statement that clarifies why both qualitative and quantitative methods are needed. Don't wait until the writing phase to do so; think about the rationale for intentionally using mixed methods as a basis for healthy discussion with your team or supervising professor. Chapter 1 in this book presents many reasons researchers choose mixed methods, but researchers do not always state these reasons in writing. It is important to describe how mixed methods fits the research topic better than a multimethod or a single-method quantitative or qualitative study.

At first blush, a rationale for mixed methods might seem obvious, but the rationale may need adjustments to make it intentional (Levitt, 2020). Without a clear rationale for using mixed methods, the methods can appear disjointed. As a result, it might be difficult for a reader to follow the logic behind using mixed methods. If you're working in a team, talking about the rationale up front will help people with different areas of expertise come together and work as a research team.

Published Example

Rashid and Iguchi (2019) provided a rationale statement early in their published article, explaining why a mixed methods design was necessary. They argued that their mixed methods study contributes to reducing violence in society as well as violence to women in particular. Pursuant to this rationale, they further argued that this mixed methods study served as the first of its kind in their home country. Their reasoning was that quantitative research alone might show how widespread a practice is, but explaining the reasons and repercussions of these practices required a qualitative component.

> The information garnered in this study can be used as an important strategy to eliminate female genital cutting (FGC) in Malaysia . . . [This is the] first study to use mixed methods study design in Malaysia on FGC. Mixed method gives better insight to the study topic. . . . The qualitative component of the study included in-depth interviews with traditional midwives (known as Mak Bidan in Malay) practising or had practised FGC in these two states. Focus group discussions were also conducted in one conveniently selected village. . . . Because no such study has been conducted in Malaysia, a questionnaire . . . was created and used by three trained research assistants in the participants' homes or place of work. (pp. 1–3)

Reflection Questions

As you craft a rationale for your mixed methods project, ask yourself the following questions:

- What is the rationale for using mixed methods for my research topic, as opposed to a multimethod or a single-method (quantitative or qualitative) research design?

- How does using mixed methods pioneer or break new ground in a specific research area?

DESIGN ESSENTIAL 3: DUAL STUDY AIMS

Dual study aims build on intentional rationale. They help define the project at the outset and then are developed for the human subjects protocol application (a formal procedure for receiving permission to conduct research) as well as for future conference presentations and manuscript preparation. Usually, people draw on their own intuition and hunches (Morse, 2010) and then refine the study aims to show the necessity of both measurement (quantitative) and experiential storytelling (qualitative) methods. In the past, textbooks emphasized issuing either a quantitative or qualitative purpose statement. However, both aspects are important in mixed methods designs, and the current convention is to outline explicitly how each method will play a contributing role in the mixed methods study (Levitt et al., 2018).

"Aims statement" is another way to say "purpose statement." The aims or purpose statement lets the reader know the topic as well as what will be measured (quantitative strand) and what will be coded and interpreted (qualitative strand). The aims statement should ideally be written in one clear sentence (Edmonson & Irby, 2008). Some statements are declarative (Johnson & Christensen, 2008) or exploratory, focusing on emerging or discoverable data. A research, grant, or thesis/dissertation proposal usually uses future language: "The purpose of this mixed methods study will be to. . . ." However, for the final defense of a thesis or dissertation, after data collection and analysis, or in a manuscript for publication, past tense is used: "The purpose of this mixed methods study was to . . ."

Published Example

In this description of the aims of the study, Singh (2019) reinforced the concept of objectivity by balancing the dual emphasis on challenges as well as affordances, or "what worked best" for students. Instead of looking only for what worked well, Singh tried to look for evidence of both sides of the coin, so to speak. As a result, Singh's aims statement clarifies the need for both measurement and an exploratory, emergent aspect:

> The desired aims of this study were not solely to measure change but to also discover how anti-racist social work education was experienced, the challenges and barriers associated with engaging with this area of learning and identifying what worked best for students with different learning needs and experiences (Pawson & Tilley, 1997). (pp. 635–636)

Reflection Questions

When composing the aims or purpose statement for your mixed methods project, ask yourself the following questions:

- What is the simplest, most direct way to state the aims of the mixed methods project, relating back to solving the research problem?

- What are the quantitative aims (e.g., to measure change) and the qualitative aims (e.g., to understand experience), and how are they balanced?

DESIGN ESSENTIAL 4: DISCUSSION OF GAPS IN SINGLE-STUDY RESEARCH AND IN THE LITERATURE

Mixed methods researchers synthesize past research, similar to creating literature reviews in single-method studies. A discussion of methodological gaps exposes unforeseen issues, such as an overreliance on quantitative surveys. In a well-written literature synthesis, authors demonstrate how their mixed methods study extends the field both methodologically and practically. They start by noting the methods used in each study and then specify the overall design (mixed methods, quantitative, or qualitative). For mixed methods designs, authors identify the type of design, such as sequential (mixed methods), and the types of data analysis, such as factor analysis and regression (quantitative survey) and thematic analysis (qualitative).

While initial forays into library databases can include listing resources, digitally annotating articles, and/or drawing literature review maps (see Creswell, 2003), a synthesis of studies goes beyond an annotated bibliography. A good basic strategy is to keep a spreadsheet tracking the database terms used in a search as well as the results and your interpretation of them. Table 2.2 presents an example including two terms, but you can use more. Be flexible and experiment with the number of terms and how they are combined.

Attention to the type of methods used in past studies will enable you to substantiate claims about whether your specific mixed methods design has previously been used to study your research topic. For example, it might be more common in a field for researchers to use quantitative studies rather than qualitative studies, or vice versa. That's why it's advantageous to articulate in the literature review section the specific benefit of contributing mixed methods studies to a corresponding field. In theses and dissertations, for example, the second chapter commonly includes a review of the literature and summarizes the state of a field. It's not uncommon for researchers to pull

TABLE 2.2. Example Literature Synthesis Spreadsheet

Database search terms	Complete citation	Methods used			Field	Key results	Strengths	Weaknesses
		Mixed methods? (Indicate specific design)	Quantitative? (Indicate specific methods and analyses)	Qualitative? (Indicate specific methods and analyses)				
Term 1	Use APA style				Describe the field	Briefly summarize relevant results	Perceived affordances of the methods	Perceived drawbacks of the methods
Term 2 (Add on additional search terms as necessary)								

Note. APA = American Psychological Association.

literature from multiple fields and then explain how the previous studies each contribute to the mixed methods design. To learn how to conduct a literature review, you may want to consult textbooks in this area—see Creswell (2003) for an introduction and Heyvaert et al. (2017) for advanced mixed methods approaches to research syntheses and literature reviews.

Jot down your impressions of the potential drawbacks of the methods of previous studies so that you can show how you would address the gap(s) in your own work. Reflect on the perceived affordance of the method(s) that were used (see Table 2.2). In your literature search, you might strike gold and come across a high-quality mixed methods study published in your field. If so, use it as an exemplar for articulating your design and keep it as a guidepost to reference as you progress with data collection and analysis efforts.

Published Example

Parke et al. (2021) explained three ways that they extended the literature on organizational behavior using mixed methods. First, they pointed out that quantitative analyses are common in studies on organizational citizen behavior, with respect to various antecedents explaining outcomes. Second, they discussed how they crafted and employed organizational interventions. Third, they explained how interviews were used in a complementary fashion to better understand the effects of these organizational change behavior (OCB) interventions:

> We extend this work by highlighting how interventions can be developed to create *equilibrium shifts* in OCB over time, or more lasting changes in the average tendencies of employees to engage in OCB (Methot et al., 2017) . . . we contribute to an ongoing debate about how supervisors and peers can affect OCB (e.g., Chen, Takeuchi, & Shum, 2013; Yaffe & Kark, 2011). Unlike previous studies, which can characterize either supervisors or peers as more effective motivators of OCB (Lemoine, Parsons, & Kansara, 2015), we demonstrate that it is useful to explicitly factor in time and consider when each party is more influential as a change agent (initial flux vs. later consolidation). (p. 1715, italics in original)

Reflection Questions

As you synthesize relevant literature to state methodological and conceptual gaps, ask yourself the following questions:

• How do the methodological gaps in single-method studies inform my mixed methods design?

- What are the key results, perceived affordances, and drawbacks of the methods used in prior studies (mixed methods, quantitative, or qualitative)?

- What exemplar studies employ the particular mixed methods design I'm using?

DESIGN ESSENTIAL 5: A THEORY-ANCHORED STUDY

How do theories anchor mixed methods research? A theory or a related set of theories presented in the literature review are key to shaping the selection of quantitative measures and qualitative protocols. A theory is a set of statements that describe, account for, or indicate the relationship(s) among concepts, phenomena, or constructs (Jaccard & Jacoby, 2010). Many research scientists and educational researchers aim to build and apply their own practical models for improving people's lives (applied research), and these models are driven by larger, arguably more universal theories (basic research).

The ways to use theory depend on the type of research. In qualitative research, theoretical frameworks undergird the design, research, and interview questions (protocols) as well as approaches to interacting with participants. Some qualitative research is meant to create psychological and social theories using a bottom-up approach, such as grounded theory, which moves from substantive (specific) to formal theory (general; Glaser & Strauss, 1967). Theories are used differently in quantitative research: As theories are tested, the results either support or do not support the theory and suggest possible modifications or additions to the initial theory.

Typically, quantitative researchers use visual diagrams to hypothesize relationships among variables when they are testing an established theory or proposing a new theory. The diagrams specify the independent variables, intervening variables (moderating or mediating), and dependent variables. If control and experimental groups are used, they are also described. Qualitative researchers use Venn diagrams, process diagrams with arrows, and other ways to represent the relationships among concepts, people, and conditions nested within cases or over periods of time.

Social justice theory is an example of a theory that can be applied to mixed methods research projects, for example engaging in transformative community research with Indigenous partners (Cram & Mertens, 2015). In this example, a satellite or cluster of theories including feminist theory, Indigenous theory, disability rights theory, and critical theory inform the study. These theories guide the researchers' positionality (see Chapter 1) to be responsive to aspirations of marginalized groups through mixed methods research.

Published Example

Manansingh et al. (2019) selected a theory of caring in their mixed methods study examining the effects of relaxation techniques on first-year baccalaureate nursing students. The quantitative strand used measures of academic stress, test anxiety, and intention to stay in the nursing profession; the qualitative strand used focus groups to unpack the students' experiences. The researchers positioned the theory of caring as an important calling for nursing and established its central importance in the study:

> Watson (1988) is a nursing theorist who focused on the theory of human caring. This theory developed from her own study in a doctoral program. Watson discussed how nurses can guide students from carative [factors] to caritas [a deeper level of "carative"], which is the result of developing the student in the academic setting and continuing the application to the clinical setting. (pp. 534–535)

In terms of the results of the study, the theory bore out the quantitative findings, indicating reduced stress due to the intervention and hence retention in the nursing program to deliver care. The qualitative findings reflected the nurses' fear about delivering care.

Reflection Questions

When describing an anchor theory (or set of theories) for your mixed methods project, ask yourself the following questions:

- What anchor theory guides both selecting quantitative measures and crafting the qualitative protocols?

- Looking forward, how do I anticipate the study results will contribute to the original theory that I cite in the literature review/synthesis?

- How might theory anchor the mixed methods project to develop a new model for applied practice?

DESIGN ESSENTIAL 6: A COMBINATION OF RESEARCH QUESTIONS, HYPOTHESES, AND/OR MIXED METHODS RESEARCH QUESTIONS

To develop the research questions, begin by wording them in a simple way, using layperson terms as if you are splashing paint to create broad strokes that can later be erased or painted over. Change the questions as needed;

be flexible. Typically, researchers use a revision process in which the research questions are refined several times. During revisions, attention to the verbs and to the order and placement of words becomes heightened. With patience, you'll end up with questions that are parsimonious in nature (meaning only the essential words are used) and that specify the qualitative and quantitative methods. You may notice that some published mixed methods studies refrain from providing research questions; however, it remains important to include them in the research process and in publications to guide the reader to connect the results to the questions.

Gay et al. (2009) provided one such example, elaborated in Table 2.3. It shows the progression from a broad research question to a narrow research question to a mixed methods research question. Note that the broad research question does not imply the type of method—it shows general inquiry. As the research question is narrowed, the quantitative and qualitative components emerge. At this stage, it may not be clear as to whether the project will be a mixed methods or a single-method study. The final mixed methods research question includes both a quantitative and a qualitative strand.

There are many approaches for formulating research questions, hypotheses, a combination of both research questions and hypotheses, or a specific mixed methods research question. For example, mixed methods researchers might include a qualitative research question and a quantitative research question and then pose a mixed methods research question showing the comparison of the quantitative data with the qualitative data. A mixed methods research question promotes methodological compatibility because it sets up a Results section that describes and then purposefully integrates the data sets. Sometimes researchers create overarching umbrella research questions that also include smaller or supplemental research questions (Morse, 2010).

TABLE 2.3. Mixed Methods Research Question Development

Broad research question	Narrow research question	Mixed methods research question
How is passing through Piaget's four stages of cognitive development related to success at college?	What factors affect the length of time children take to pass from one Piagetian stage to the next?	What factors (quantitative strand) and experiences (qualitative strand) inform students' progression through Piaget's four stages of cognitive development that determine college success?

Published Example 1: Multiple Research Questions

Using an explanatory sequential design, Shelton et al. (2020) posed three research questions to investigate the role of resilience and spirituality in executive leaders' stress. They used a combination of open-ended qualitative questions and closed-ended quantitative questions to describe how they will first assess resilience, well-being, stressors, and life satisfaction (quantitative strand) and then to interview executives (qualitative strand):

> RQ [Research question] 1. What are the differences in the resilience of spiritually oriented leaders compared to the general population? (quantitative strand)
>
> RQ 2. Are the type and frequency of spiritual practice related to leader resilience? (quantitative strand)
>
> RQ 3. How do spiritual practices relate to a leader's sense of psychological well-being and life satisfaction? (qualitative strand) (p. 402)

Published Example 2: Umbrella Research Question With Supplemental Research Questions

Morse (2010) constructed an umbrella (main) qualitative research question with supplemental quantitative research questions. This question positions the qualitative strand as core to the mixed methods study:

> RQ: What is the experience of stigma in the doctor–patient relationship when patients who smoke are undergoing treatment for lung cancer? [qualitative strand: interview data] (p. 210)

For the quantitative strand, Morse used the notation system "S1" for Strand 1 and "S2" for Strand 2:

> RQ S1: What is the duration of the physician–patient visit, from the time the physician enters the room until he or she leaves? [quantitative strand: observations]
>
> RQ S2: Are there differences in the filing claims for asbestos-related lung cancer between smoker and nonsmokers? [quantitative strand: recorded physician data] (p. 212)

Published Example 3: Research Questions That Shape Hypotheses

Brett et al. (2002) described a qualitative ethnographic phase that would be used to develop a quantitative health intervention. Therefore, they chose to use open-ended research questions. For the intervention, they described how they planned to switch to using hypotheses to test the effects of the intervention:

RQ 1: What factors and values operate at the family and community level that might explain the relatively low levels of physical activity and fruit and vegetable consumption and the relatively high levels of poor health outcomes correlated with these patterns?

RQ 2: What efforts on the individual, family, and community levels would likely succeed in making necessary changes by working collaboratively with the community? . . . This approach provides us a period of hypothesis development using an explicitly inductive approach with the intention of deductively testing resulting hypotheses. This gives us the opportunity to approach the proposed intervention with freshness and new ideas. A client-driven approach seeks to identify the opportunities in peoples' lives where change can be made and to develop an attitude of partnership with participant families and the community. (p. 332)

Published Example 4: Hypotheses

Hypotheses are generally less common in mixed methods research articles than in quantitative research articles. For example, Kim and Lim (2013, p. 1166) started by posing a general research question, "Will middle-grade females' and Latinos' reactions to an embodied agent be qualitatively different from Caucasian males' reactions?" and then broke their inquiry into four hypotheses. The hypotheses formed the anchor for the study because the researchers were interested in group differences, compared along various dependent measures:

1. Females and Latino students would evaluate their agent more positively than Caucasian males;

2. Females' and Latinos' attitudes toward learning mathematics from their agent would be more positive than Caucasian males' attitudes;

3. Females' and Latinos' self-efficacy in learning mathematics from their agent would be higher than Caucasian males' self-efficacy; and

4. Females and Latinos would increase their learning similar to Caucasian males after the intervention. (Kim & Lim, 2013, p. 1166)

Published Example 5: Mixed Methods Research Question

With so many possible research questions in a mixed methods project, it can be helpful to parse them out individually to keep the study organized and connected. For example, Parey (2019) chose to group the questions by method, ending with a specific mixed methods research question. Keeping with more recent trends in the mixed methods research field, the mixed methods research question emphasized how the data would be integrated, or compared, in a separate analysis and presented in a separate results section (p. 201).

Quantitative Research Questions

1. What are primary and secondary school teachers' attitudes towards the inclusion for children with disabilities in inclusive schools?

2. What are primary and secondary school teachers' attitudes towards the inclusion of children with various disability types?

3. What are primary and secondary school teachers' concerns regarding the inclusion of children with disabilities?

4. What are primary and secondary school teachers' perceived self-efficacy regarding the inclusion of children with disabilities?

5. What are the variables associated with primary and secondary school teachers' attitudes, concerns, and perceived self-efficacy?

6. To what extent do overall attitudes, concerns, and perceived self-efficacy differ between primary and secondary school teachers?

Qualitative Research Questions

1. What are the reasons for the overall attitudes towards the inclusion of children with disabilities in inclusive schools among primary school teachers?

2. What are the reasons for the overall attitudes towards the inclusion of children with disabilities in inclusive schools among secondary school teachers?

3. Are there any differences in reasons among both teacher types?

Mixed Methods Research Question

1. How can the integrated quantitative and qualitative results provide more insight into teachers' attitudes? (Parey, 2019, p. 201)

Reflection Questions

As you design your research questions and/or hypotheses, ask yourself the following questions:

- What is my basic, broad research question?
- How will I break down the basic research question into qualitative and quantitative research questions or hypotheses?
- For the quantitative data, is a hypothesis more suitable than a research question?
- What mixed methods research question integrates both the qualitative and quantitative research question(s)?

DESIGN ESSENTIAL 7: ONE OR TWO SAMPLING STAGES

What makes sampling in mixed methods studies different than in single-method studies? Sampling in mixed methods projects can occur at one or more stages. For example, sequential and experimental/intervention mixed methods studies use two stages of sampling: The first sampling stage is to establish the initial sample for a quantitative strand (say, surveys), and the second sampling stage is to determine which participants will serve as the sample for the qualitative strand (say, interviews). Some might call this sample a "qualitative subsample" of the first, larger quantitative sample. By definition, quantitative and qualitative sampling strategies are different. Sampling follows general qualitative guidelines (convenient or purposefully selected groups), quantitative rules (using a random group based on certain selection criteria to represent a larger population), or a combination therein.

Random sampling is selecting participants so that every member has an equal chance of being selected; it is used when the researchers want to generalize the findings (Graziano & Raulin, 2013). Researchers may use automatic random number generators or tables of random numbers. Stratified random sampling involves grouping participants by subpopulations, such as age, race, gender, occupation, organization, or geographical region. The key to this strategy is to make sure that the number of people in each sample subgroup reflects the number in the larger population. For example, you might use the U.S. Census data to determine the distribution of your target groups in the larger population and then select stratified random samples based on proportionate numbers. Other strategies can be found in research methods textbooks.

In qualitative research, nonprobabilistic sampling strategies—purposefully selecting participants based on certain criteria—are used instead of the probabilistic random sampling strategies common to quantitative research. For example, in purposive or purposeful sampling (Patton, 2002), the research team selects participants based on their "information-rich" qualities (p. 46). Purposive sampling thus differs from stratified random sampling because it does not aim to reflect the larger population.

Another form of nonprobabilistic sampling is convenient sampling (Patton, 2002), which is often used in mixed methods studies that examine the experiences of an existing group of people enrolled in a specific class, health clinic, or other type of program. Other strategies for sampling are maximal variation sampling (Glaser & Strauss, 1967), snowball sampling (Morgan, 2008), and community or peer nomination sampling (Cillessen & Marks, 2017).

See Miles and Huberman (1994) for a typology of sampling strategies in qualitative inquiry.

Sampling is an important way to integrate and coherently link the quantitative strand of a mixed method study with the qualitative strand. For example, one might purposively sample survey respondents based on enrollment in a class. Once the survey data have been analyzed, at least preliminarily, then some of the respondents might be contacted, based on their responses or demographics, for a follow-up interview or focus group (e.g., Zieber & Sedgewick, 2018). Sampling is explored further in Chapters 3, 4, and 5.

Published Example

Kim and Lim's (2013) sequential explanatory mixed methods design used two stages of sampling:

> **Stage 1 Sample for Surveys (Quantitative Strand):** Participants were one hundred twenty 9th graders enrolled in Algebra I classes in two inner-city high schools in a mountain-west state in the United States. Sixty-four students were male (53%) and fifty-six were female (47%). Sixty-one students were Caucasian (51%) and fifty-nine Latino (49%). In the participating school districts, students were able to start taking Algebra I in the seventh grade and required to complete it by the ninth grade. Thus, the participants who had delayed the course until required were assumed to be less interested in mathematics than the rest of the ninth graders in the schools. The average age of the participants was 15.93 (SD = 0.87). (p. 3)

> **Stage 2 Sample for Interviews (Qualitative Strand):** The interviews were focused on a deeper understanding of the females' experiences and the clear contrast between Latinas' and Caucasian males' reactions. Initially, 12 interviewees were randomly selected from the participant pool that had completed both lessons, which resulted in a sample of eight Caucasian males, two Caucasian females, and two Latinas. A second round of sampling was conducted to obtain a theoretical sample (six to eight) from each comparison group, to ensure a meaningful, thematic analysis. The sampling targeted the two female groups, from which six Caucasian females and four Latinas were further selected randomly. (p. 6)

Reflection Questions

As you select samples, ask yourself the following questions:

- What is my sampling strategy for the first strand, phase, or wave of data in my mixed methods project?

- Do I use the same sampling strategy to collect the second strand of data, or do I need to construct a secondary (smaller) subsample from the primary sample?

DESIGN ESSENTIAL 8: A MIXED METHODS DIAGRAM

Unlike in single-study research projects, it's common practice in mixed methods projects to provide a visual diagram that represents the mixed method design. Why are visual diagrams important in mixed methods research? Visual diagrams help the reader track the strands, phases, or waves of data. And, as discussed in Chapter 1, a diagram serves as a touchstone for understanding the gestalt, or totality of the project, which is especially useful when a mixed methods research project involves several team members. Basically, the diagram helps to chart and plan the qualitative and quantitative strands of the project. Chapter 7 also includes discussion of why diagrams are great for presentation, publication, and grant applications.

As you consider the designs laid out in the chapters that follow, you'll want to prioritize a quantitative or qualitative strand, or both. As mentioned in Chapter 1, historically the quantitative strand of a mixed methods project was considered more dominant or was prioritized vis-à-vis the qualitative strand (sequential explanatory or experimental mixed methods designs). But now, the qualitative strand might be prioritized (see Morse, 2010). Not only does one type of strand typically come before the other in terms of chronological order, but the data are privileged in terms of the main results. Sometimes, both strands are considered equal status and collected at the same time (concurrent).

Variations in Diagramming and Notating

Much the same way that visual diagrams enjoy a history in both qualitative and quantitative social sciences to explain relationships among concepts, mixed methods diagrams are used to clarify phases of a project over time. For instance, temporal and conditional processes are used in grounded theory diagrams (Glaser & Strauss, 1967). Mathematical modeling plots variables on graphs to explore relationships as well as to explain structural and measurement models (Jaccard & Jacoby, 2010). Other mixed methods diagrams explain content validity, how well the measures reflect the concept intended to be measured. Some diagrams describe how theory informs each phase of a mixed methods project and chart how data influence the development of a phase of a mixed methods project (see Newman et al., 2013). Chapters 3, 4, and 5 present more details about each mixed methods design, selecting a design, and producing a representational visual diagram. Notation systems can also be used to demarcate the order of each qualitative ("Qual") and quantitative ("Quan") strand. For example, Nastasi et al. (2007) discussed several mixed methods approaches and notated which strand comes first: "Qual →/+ Quan →/+ Qual →/+ Quan . . . Qual →/+ Quan, or Qual →← Quan" (p. 164).

Example

Figure 2.1 shows a visual diagram that breaks down the quantitative strand and the qualitative strand of a convergent mixed methods design. Note that both strands occur simultaneously, without priority status. The type of data and corresponding procedures are briefly described at each stage.

Reflection Questions

As you diagram your mixed methods design, ask yourself the following questions:

- Would I start the diagram with either a qualitative or quantitative strand, or both?

- What quantitative data do I want to "explain" with qualitative data (if any)?

- What qualitative phenomenon do I want to "explore" to then shape the quantitative phase (if any)?

- Which symbols (e.g., squares, circles, ovals) in the diagram would represent the study phases in a clear manner?

DESIGN ESSENTIAL 9: ETHICAL COLLABORATIONS WITH THE RESEARCH SITE AND PARTICIPANTS

In addition to the team-building principles outlined in Chapter 1, mixed methods research requires several formal, ethical tasks. To start, anticipate the need to get site permission letters before data collection as part of liaising

FIGURE 2.1. Visual Diagram (Convergent or Parallel Design)

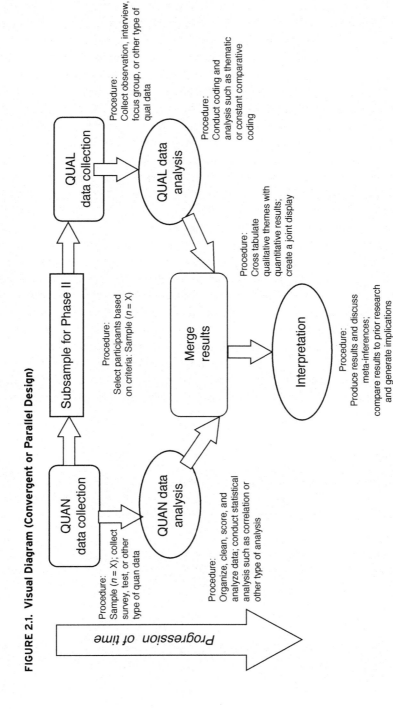

with the research site and for submitting a human subjects protocol. Assuring the ethical treatment of study participants, called "human subjects," through Institutional Review Board (IRB) approval is mandatory for conducting social science research, including mixed methods research (whether for theses, dissertations, or other studies). IRB approval is mandatory to protect study participants from possible harm as well as to explain study participation guidelines clearly. This process upholds the mixed methods design principle of understanding multiple truths because it reflects multiple interpretations of the inherent value of a research project. Beneficence (weighing the risks and benefits to participants), autonomy (the right to decide to participate in research), and justice (equal access to risks and benefits) are the guiding ethical principles for research with human subjects (Graziano & Raulin, 2013).

Accordingly, all researchers, including faculty members, clinicians, research assistants, and students, are required to complete training on research ethics to qualify to submit a human subjects protocol, consent participants, and collect and analyze data. Community partners who do not handle or work with the data may not be required to obtain research training. Consult with the research office at your institution to learn more about research with populations characterized as vulnerable, including minors/children, people with intellectual and/or physical disabilities, pregnant people, immigrants, and people who are incarcerated. Benefits of mixed methods research studies to participants and to society may include improving educational or health outcomes, voicing opinions, experiencing relief, and forming community (Mustanski et al., 2017).

Published Example

Researchers indicate that their studies are approved by Institutional Review Boards. This establishes credibility and shows research integrity. For example, McMahon et al. (2021) included in their paper the following:

> Ethics and dissemination: The study was approved by the University of Rochester Institutional Review Board (RSRB00052766). Study findings will be disseminated to community members and providers and to researchers and policy makers. (p. 1)

Reflection Questions

As you consider ethical requirements for your project, ask yourself the following questions:

- What is the process for submitting the human subjects protocol?

- If working with community partner(s), is there a separate organizational review process for granting permission to conduct research in addition to the university Institutional Review Board?

Participant Recruitment

Mixed methods studies describe, recruit, and enroll participants. Researchers may use a statistical process known as power analysis to estimate the number of participants needed in the quantitative phase of the study to allow inferences to the population at large (see Wiedmaier, 2017). Power analysis is often calculated prior to starting research.

In addition to power analysis, the details of the study site (geographical location) and context (organization) and participants' background demographics are described. Mixed methods research projects vary as to the extent participants are described. Typically, demographic data are collected about study participants after recruitment and after they consent to participate. However, some projects provide further detail about relevant characteristics, especially medical studies or educational studies in which a case strategy is used.

Recruitment refers to efforts to advertise the study via outreach into various communities. Equitable opportunities to enroll in the study are important for ensuring access to the study especially in underserved communities who may not have easy and direct access to researchers.

Published Example

McMahon et al. (2021) conducted a mixed methods study investigating transmission of human immunodeficiency virus (HIV). They described the numerous social media outlets and organizations they contacted to fairly recruit an appropriate sample for the study:

> Recruitment efforts focused on increasing awareness of the study among HIV different heterosexual couples in the New York City area by employing five primary methods: (1) distribution of study posters and pamphlets (Figure 2); (2) passive referrals from clinics, service agencies and community-based organisations; (3) social media campaign (Facebook, Twitter, Craigslist; project website); (4) traditional advertisements in newspapers, magazines, subway signs and radio; and (5) peer-referral with a maximum of three referrals per enrolled couple. These methods directed those interested in the study to contact study staff directly by calling a toll-free phone number, text messaging, emailing or accessing the study website to obtain further information and

undergo initial eligibility screening. Those who met the eligibility criteria were offered assistance for informing and recruiting their primary partner into the study using strategies developed by Witte and colleagues. (p. 3)

Reflection Questions

As you consider the ethical tasks necessary for your project, ask yourself the following questions:

- What is the process for submitting the human subjects protocol?

- If working with community partner(s), is there a separate organizational review process for granting permission to conduct research in addition to the university IRB?

- How will I collect and describe participant demographic and background data?

- Do I need to conduct a power analysis to determine the number of participants for the sample in the quantitative strand?

- What are the best ways to recruit and enroll participants in the study?

DESIGN ESSENTIAL 10: A COMPREHENSIVE DESCRIPTION OF QUANTITATIVE MEASURES AND QUALITATIVE DATA PROTOCOLS

The selection of data collection methods is tied to the research questions. Diagramming your mixed methods design will help you play around with, and ultimately decide on, the type and number of measures and qualitative protocols. Table 2.4 outlines common data collection measures and protocols. Depending on the type of design you select (see Chapters 3, 4, and 5), you will likely explore the sequence and timing of data collection.

Operationalizing what you want to study centers on breaking down a construct into quantitative variables and qualitative concepts. Table 2.5 shows ways to operationalize the study of creativity and to narrow the options for studying this construct. Three examples of quantitative variables and three examples of qualitative concepts are included. Depending on the study design, each variable can be independent or dependent. Operationalizing the construct is a critical yet overlooked step, especially in mixed methods studies—you don't want one strand to study one thing and another strand to study a different thing if you initially thought you were studying the same thing.

TABLE 2.4. Qualitative and Quantitative Data Collection Options

Data	Types	Data files	Potential affordances	Potential drawbacks
Qualitative (words)				
Interviews	Structured, semistructured, unstructured (individual, dyadic, group)	Audio transcription	Verbal representation of thoughts, feelings, beliefs through responding to questions posed in real-time	Amount of time Rapport required to support validity in responses
Focus groups	Structured Community-based	Audio transcription	Oral/linguistic group-mediated opinions, perspectives, and experiences	Group influences discussion and alters opinions
Observations	Participant, semiparticipant, complete observer	Field notes Video	Real-world phenomena and events, immersion in-situ	Requires field visits Challenging to take notes while observing
Documents and records	Speeches, journals, diaries, autobiographies, archives, minutes, physician records, student data, census data	Digital Hand-written	In-depth written descriptions of experiences and events by participants	Considered as supporting, not primary, evidence; federal regulations prohibit access to private records
Web-based data	Blogs, websites, social media platforms, emails	Digital	Posts are evidence of discourse or disclosure of information	Permission required if not publicly available
Works of art	Photographs, paintings, dance, theatre, music performances	Photographs or videos of original work	Access to creative self-expression as represented through symbol systems such as color, movement, sound, and inter-actions including play	Challenging to capture artistic process Hard to discern meaning of the artwork as intended by the artist or maker

(continues)

TABLE 2.4. Qualitative and Quantitative Data Collection Options (Continued)

Data	Types	Data files	Potential affordances	Potential drawbacks
		Quantitative (numbers)		
Surveys	A validated set of questions or statement to which participants rate the extent of agreement	Electronic or paper	Numerical data on thoughts, feelings, knowledge, attitudes, behaviors	Self-report data are subjective; Self-ratings may change over time
Scales and measures	Short or long form; Performance measures; Attitudinal measures	Electronic or paper	Self-report or performance data using large data sets from a variety of subgroups of a population	Might be normed on majority populations; Incentivization of participation may be an obstacle
Physiological data	Electroencephalogram; magnetic resonance imaging	Electronic	Diverse physiological data	Time intensive and labor-intensive; Facilities and equipment can be expensive or hard to obtain
Behavioral observations	Behavioral scales; Behavioral checklists	Electronic or paper	Recordings of intervention-based or naturalistic situational behavior	Physical set up of activities as well as access to participants can be challenging
Tests of perception	Tests that examine visual, spatial perception, speech, etc.	Electronic or paper	Standardized tests that evaluate the ability to process information in different ways	Like many tests, requires skilled trained professional and can be resource intensive
Geographic data	Maps that indicate locations, migration, etc.	Electronic or paper	Specific information	Can require special technology, potentially expensive

TABLE 2.5. Operationalizing a Construct and Defining an Investigatory Concept for a Mixed Methods Study

Construct	Quantitative variable	Quantitative measure	Qualitative concept	Qualitative method
Creativity	Divergent thinking	Alternate Uses Test (Guilford, 1966)	Thoughts about creativity	Interviews
	Creative achievement	Creative Achievement Questionnaire (Carson et al., 2005)	Group goals about creativity	Focus groups
	Beliefs about creativity	Self-Report Beliefs About Creativity survey (Hass et al., 2016)	Intentions and motivations informing invention-behavior	Classroom observation

Collecting data involves interacting with participants who have consented to participate. Researchers ask potential participants to read and sign the proper consent forms, after which the participants take part in the research tasks, such as interventions or interviews. Researchers use research standards of practice to ensure trust, rapport, and professionalism. These standards promote integrity and proper handling of data to preserve confidentiality and anonymity.

Data files range in type and size, and organization is key to housing and storing data on an institution-approved server and/or approved cloud-based software program. Developing a good method for storing files using numbers or pseudonyms to represent participants is key. It's also important to think about the confidentiality of the data files. Only qualified study personnel should have access to stored files.

Published Example

Segers et al. (2019) conducted a convergent mixed methods study on the topic of family empowerment using a rating scale coupled with interviews about each item of that scale:

> The Dutch Family Empowerment Scale (FES) is a 24-item rating scale that provides insight into parents' sense of their own empowerment at one particular point in time. It consists of two domains: family and service systems. The FES covers three expressions of empowerment: attitudes, knowledge, and behaviours. The FES has been translated into various languages, including Dutch. (p. 112)

To give insight into the comprehensiveness and comprehensibility of the FES, analysis of the interviews was carried out following the method described by

Knafl et al. (2007). This method takes the individual item as a basis for the analysis and distinguishes between interpretations and issues that participants made regarding the items. (p. 114)

Reflection Questions

As you reflect on describing and collecting data, ask yourself the following questions:

- How does the data collection tie back to the research questions and type of mixed methods design?
- Which quantitative measures best represent the quantitative strand?
- Which qualitative data protocols best represent the qualitative strand?

SUMMARY

Chapter 2 clarified that mixed methods research is an outgrowth of single-method research, with similar properties, but has evolved over recent years into a distinctive methodology spanning many fields with 10 core design essentials. Armed with the knowledge of these 10 core design essentials, published examples, and reflection questions, you can now more clearly make mixed methods design decisions, resulting in a strong mixed methods project. Your design might depend on other issues such as access to research sites, the goals of your research partners, or participant availability. The next three chapters will give you a more in-depth understanding of the difference between mixed methods designs: Chapter 3 (sequential explanatory and exploratory designs), Chapter 4 (concurrent designs), and Chapter 5 (experimental designs). Let's jump into sequential mixed methods designs, contrasting explanatory with exploratory.

3 SEQUENTIAL MIXED METHODS DESIGNS

Now that you've learned 10 essential features of high-quality mixed methods design, let's dive into arguably the most common type of design—the sequential mixed methods design. A great metaphor for sequential designs that start with either quantitative or qualitative methods—such as a survey and an interview protocol—is a tandem bicycle, which is a two-seated bike. Together, two bicyclists work to power the bike uphill or balance down tricky turns. Similarly, both quantitative and qualitative data are needed to make a sequential mixed methods project. Some sequential mixed methods projects start with quantitative data or qualitative data. Just as the bicyclist in the front is the lead, steering and influencing the reactions of the bicyclist behind, the first type of data collected in a sequential design steers the collection of the second type of data. In this chapter, we consider how the qualitative and the quantitative data—though collected separately at different time points in stages—work in tandem.

https://doi.org/10.1037/0000404-004

How to Mix Methods: A Guide to Sequential, Convergent, and Experimental Research Designs, by J. Katz-Buonincontro

Chapter 3 leads you through both explanatory and exploratory sequential mixed methods studies, in which quantitative and qualitative methods work in tandem with each other. These designs contrast with convergent designs, in which data are typically collected simultaneously (see Chapter 4), and with experimental mixed methods designs, which use one or more intervention groups and a control group and include a qualitative interview (see Chapter 5). The major steps for crafting your sequential mixed methods projects are provided. Design questions offer you a way to reflect on further development of each step. Exemplar studies provide a sense of the ways in which researchers design their projects to answer research questions and sample participants at each stage.

EXPLANATORY SEQUENTIAL DESIGNS

Sequential designs differ slightly depending on the field, the use of mixed methods reporting conventions, and the needs of stakeholders (clients, communities, programs). For example, not all studies use a positionality stance, a mixed methods diagram, or a joint display, as advocated in Chapter 2. However, it's still a good practice to develop these essential design features. Even if journals do not permit space for inclusion of these elements, it's helpful to include them for future journal articles or presentations, which I discuss further in Chapter 7. Also, sequential designs are different from experimental designs that focus on an intervention; experimental designs are discussed in Chapter 5. Let's unpack how qualitative methods are used to explain quantitative results in explanatory sequential designs.

Qualitative Explanation of Quantitative Results

What is an explanatory sequential mixed methods design? Explanatory sequential mixed methods designs emphasize a qualitative explanation of quantitative results. These designs often include a survey followed by an interview or other type of qualitative data collection method such as a focus group (cf. Goodwin et al., 2018). The purpose of the qualitative data is to explain and hence expand on the quantitative data.

Explanatory sequential designs are arguably the most popular type of mixed methods design. Why are they so popular? This design can be appealing because it is a comprehensive way to gather a large amount of opinion-focused data, for example by using surveys to elicit individual opinions from groups of people in an organization or community, and then to focus on aspects of that data, such as specific explanations of those opinions, with smaller groups of people.

All sorts of research problems can be examined with explanatory sequential designs: inequities, learning problems, disease, therapeutic challenges, and unknown effects of interventions, for example (see Chapter 5 for more information on experimental mixed methods designs). Rationales for using sequential mixed methods explanatory designs include wanting to better understand a certain phenomenon or set of facts as exposed through analysis of quantitative (numeric) data. Single-method studies may provide quantitative analyses of item variance, group-level performance on a measure, or the variables that mediate certain outcomes on a dependent measure; however, they fail to capture the "why"—why people perform a certain way, why people rate themselves a certain way, why people provide answers to a survey in a certain way. Therefore, mixed methods researchers attempt to bridge the "what" (quantitative analyses) with the "why" (qualitative analyses). Typically, the aim of a quantitative strand is described first, and then the aim of a qualitative strand is described (see Chapter 2).

Figure 3.1 provides the major steps in designing an explanatory sequential mixed methods project. While it's not uncommon for research designs to be compared to recipes or formulas following the scientific method, research projects are quite iterative. Therefore, you will likely float back and forth between the research questions and corresponding research methods as opposed to completing each step in its entirety.

Timelines for executing each phase of a project depend on fluctuating circumstances such as subject recruitment or issues like the COVID-19 pandemic that may prevent face-to-face data collection. You might change what type of quantitative data you want to collect and then adjust the research questions or hypotheses and the type of analyses (see Chapter 2, Design Essential 6). Choosing a new type of quantitative data would affect the type of qualitative data, the sample, and the interview protocol questions so they are linked to the quantitative data.

Step 1: Start With the Quantitative Strand: The "What"

Starting an explanatory sequential project with the quantitative strand might include surveys or measures. Refer to Chapter 2, Table 2.4, as you think about your research construct and possible ways to measure and assess it. The goal of Step 1 is to select a valid and reliable survey or measure to collect quantitative data before collecting qualitative data. The quantitative strand

FIGURE 3.1. Design Steps for Sequential Explanatory Mixed Methods Designs

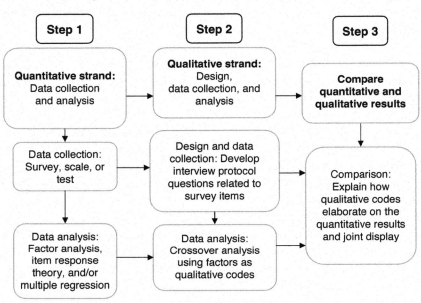

Note. While the steps are labeled to show the general sequence of the method, you may find it necessary to go back and forth during the research process.

paints a broad picture—the lay of the land, if you will. The quantitative results provide data on the current state of affairs of a particular psychological reality or social phenomenon. The quantitative data enable the reader to understand the "what" of a certain issue. Remember, you can consult Chapter 2, Table 2.5, to explore, weigh, and contemplate types of quantitative data.

Typically, quantitative data are collected and often analyzed before sequencing the qualitative strand. The reason for breaking up these two strands into stages, or phases, is to understand the quantitative data first. Then, you can start to plan to collect the qualitative data. For example, an intentional mixed methods rationale might be to explain group-level differences (quantitative) and then to understand individual-level differences (qualitative) with respect to a certain topic (cf. McCrudden & McTighe, 2019). The intentional juxtaposition of these two types of data can help address a problem better than just examining the existence of the problem (the "what"). Another example of an intentional explanatory sequential mixed methods rationale is first to establish the prevalence of practice and then to help understand the reasons, repercussions, or possible side effects (Rashid & Iguchi, 2019).

Figure 3.1 shows the three basic steps in an explanatory sequential mixed methods design. First, quantitative data collection and analysis are planned. In the example, a validated survey is first used and then analyzed in terms of factor analysis (a data-reduction approach to statistically find similarities and a structure among several questions or items) and/or item response theory (a way to examine item or question difficulty and accuracy of measurement goals). Examples of Strand 1 quantitative data are clinical files, the Connor-Davidson Resilience Scale (Connor & Davidson, 2003), and the Impact of Event Scale (IES-R; West et al., 2014); knowledge tests, the Nursing Anxiety and Self-Confidence with Clinical Decision Making tool (White, 2014), and the Nursing Student Competence Scale (Zieber & Sedgwick, 2018); or a new basic survey for an unstudied topic (Rashid & Iguchi, 2019).

Design Questions: To begin Step 1, think about the 10 design essentials of mixed methods research introduced in Chapter 1. Then, start to conceptualize the juxtaposition of the quantitative and qualitative data:

- What type of quantitative data will I collect?
- What analyses would I plan for the quantitative data?
- What are the main, interesting, or surprising quantitative results that call for further explanation with qualitative data?

Step 2: Sequence the Qualitative Strand: The "Why" or "How"

The second major step in explanatory sequential mixed methods design is the qualitative design, data collection, and analysis. Even though the qualitative strand occurs after the quantitative strand, the qualitative phase of data collection is quite important and does not necessarily have secondary status even though it is positioned after the quantitative strand. For example, an interview protocol can be developed and pilot tested to ensure it connects to the concepts represented by the survey items. The interview results can be coded using a matrix of codes based on the survey, meaning the survey factors would be used as a set of a priori codes to analyze the interview transcriptions.

As mentioned previously, the rationale for using qualitative data is to explain, describe, expand on, or elaborate on the "why" or "how" people experience the psychological reality or social phenomenon as represented by the quantitative data analysis. Articulated thoughts, beliefs, and experiences extend and possibly deepen the understanding of the measured construct. As researcher Dr. Matthew McCrudden, Professor of Education at Pennsylvania State University, stated,

> When doing quantitative research, I noticed within-group differences in the samples. Quantitative research allows us to make general statements about

a group based on group means and variability around the mean. This can be helpful for gaining a snapshot understanding of a sample. However, this is a broad-brush stroke and can miss nuances among participants. Using purposeful sampling to implement a qualitative strand to follow-up a quantitative strand can provide us a better understanding of differences within a group, and it can give us the perspectives of participants who are distinguished from the group average or are otherwise positioned on the margins. Therefore, explanatory sequential designs allow us to balance general patterns within samples and to gain deeper insights into meaningful variability within samples. (M. McCrudden, personal communication, May 5, 2023)

Qualitative data can be generated from open-ended questionnaires (Rashid & Iguchi, 2019), or interview protocols or focus groups. Interviews can be held once or at multiple time points (Zieber & Sedgewick, 2018). Researchers can choose which interview approach is best suited to the subject matter. For instance, narrative interviews focus on storytelling (Katz-Buonincontro, 2022) as to the impact of an experience, for example an injury, that was revealed through a survey (West et al., 2014).

Sampling the qualitative group can be done in a variety of ways (see also the overview of sampling in Chapter 2). Some researchers call this process "sampling integration" (McCrudden & McTighe, 2019). Keep in mind that all study participants can be recruited and invited to participate in interviews, focus groups, observations, or other activities. However, enrolling all participants might not be feasible with large samples—with large samples, a convenient qualitative sample can be selected based on those who volunteer to participate. Participants can indicate their willingness and interest to participate in the qualitative data collection on a paper or electronic survey form (e.g., Qualtrics, Survey Monkey, Google Forms).

Another sampling strategy is to select a purposive sample of people who respond in a certain way on the initial survey or measure. For example, people could be clustered to form small focus groups according to their survey responses, depending on the research questions and a clear sampling criterion. Some studies first analyze survey scores in the quantitative phase and then sample qualitative participants based on whether they had high, medium, or low scores. With surveys that might have ceiling effects, this process may not be possible. Other studies might involve selection of a qualitative sample based on the type of survey responses. For example, de Visser and McDonnell (2012) chose a stratified sample of interviewees from the larger sample of 731 survey respondents based on whether they held traditional or egalitarian gender role beliefs. The resulting purposive sample included an equal representation of eight men and eight women. The interview protocol included questions about alcohol consumption related to their gender identity as well as their socialization. Importantly, the interviewer was blind to each participant's quantitative scores so as not to influence the interview questioning process.

Additional approaches to designing the qualitative sample within the larger context of the quantitative sample include basing selection on organizational role (recruiting dyads of supervisors and direct reports), enrollment (recruiting sections of a class), or demographic variable(s) (recruiting based on ability level, gender, ethnicity, income level). Hamed et al.'s (2018) study provides an example of a focus group sampling method based on organizational role (faculty or student) as the criterion for assignment to focus groups. This sampling method helped explain the quantitative assessment of clinical competence.

Conceptual explanation is the guiding principle for shaping the qualitative protocols so they connect in a logical way to the quantitative measures and instruments. Chapter 6, focusing on integration and joint displays, covers the use of quantitative factors as a posteriori codes when examining transcriptions derived from interviews, focus groups, or qualitative observations. A posteriori codes are developed after the interview and transcription take place based on emergence of their importance to the research question(s).

Design Question: For Step 2—developing a qualitative interview, focus group, or observation protocol stemming from the quantitative results—ask yourself the following question:

• Using the principle of conceptual explanation, what qualitative interview or focus group questions encompassing lived phenomena, experiences, thought patterns, or belief systems connect to the items, factors, correlations, or predictions explained in the quantitative data analyses?

Step 3: Compare the Quantitative and Qualitative Results

It's important to write up the data analysis procedures for both the quantitative and the qualitative data sets as they are analyzed. This means defining and citing the specific qualitative coding procedure (such as cleaning and reviewing data, extracting descriptive phases, developing codes, making categories based on the codes, identifying cross-cutting themes, and peer debriefing; Katz-Buonincontro, 2022). In addition, this step includes describing the statistical analysis procedure(s) used (such as defining indicators of constructs for factor analysis, considering how many dimensions exist, and selecting items or scales to be included in a measure) as well as relevant details such as factor extraction, eigenvalues and their magnitude, factor rotation, and creating a correlation matrix (Green & Salkind, 2017).

The current writing convention in mixed methods is to include a separate third section in the Results section of an article, featuring the comparison. This section is important because it allows the researchers to try to make sense of potential commonalities or differences across the data sets. Providing sufficient details when analyzing, comparing, and integrating data is critical for maintaining a well-balanced and easily interpretable mixed methods study. A discussion of the process of comparing and integrating the results in a narrative fashion that includes a joint display or graphic representation of the results is included in Chapter 6.

Design Questions: Guiding questions for comparing the quantitative and the qualitative results include the following:

- What are the data analysis procedures that I used (qualitative and quantitative)?

- How do I characterize the nature of the correspondence between the quantitative and qualitative results—confirmatory, explanatory, convergent or divergent, discordant?

EXPLORATORY SEQUENTIAL MIXED METHODS DESIGNS

The exploratory sequential mixed methods design attempts to break new research ground. It could be used for research in an understudied or overlooked area (e.g., due to historical racism), a private or potentially sensitive area (e.g., sexual abuse), a difficult-to-reach geographic region, or a combination of these reasons. Exploratory studies flip the order of data collection used in explanatory designs. Qualitative data collection methods, such as interviews or focus groups, come first as a core approach to developing or altering and piloting a survey or instrument.

Exploratory sequential mixed methods designs are used to explore an aspect of human experience through the careful sequencing of qualitative and then quantitative data. In addition to basic educational and psychological research, the exploratory sequential mixed methods design fits culture-specific research. Computing, educational technology, digital humanities, informatics, and library science researchers who want to pilot a tool in technology and then add a quantitative survey or instrument related to that tool might also use an exploratory sequential mixed methods design. Figure 3.2 shows the steps used in exploratory sequential designs, which are described in the following sections.

FIGURE 3.2. Design Steps for Sequential Exploratory Mixed Methods Designs

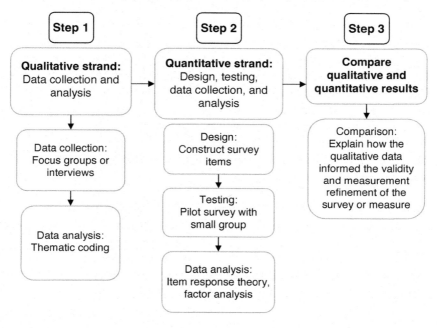

Step 1: Start With the Qualitative Strand

Exploratory sequential mixed methods studies typically start with qualitative data collection and analysis, followed by quantitative data collection and analysis.

Many exploratory designs use focus groups or interviews to explore new areas. The topics might be personally or politically sensitive, thus requiring immersive discussions obtained through posing and answering questions. Interviews allow for in-depth questions pertaining to, for example, positive or negative experiences involving health and well-being.

The sample might include groups who have not had opportunities to participate in research. The qualitative sample is typically fewer than 30 persons, though it is important to note that the sample size should be appropriate to the research questions and the context of the mixed methods research project. Interview protocol questions can be pretested with people known to have had experiences relevant to the questions, such as a group of patients with different educational levels (Jafer et al., 2021). See Katz-Buonincontro (2022) for tips on crafting open-ended, exploratory, and probing interview questions.

Exploratory sequential mixed methods designs can be appropriate for culture-specific research (Nastasi & Hitchcock, 2016) and newly researched and overlooked areas of study, such as exploring patterns of racial hyper-privilege across student racial groups (Cabrera, 2011).

An exploratory sequential mixed methods research project that purposefully adapted a quantitative questionnaire using a culturally sensitive approach was conducted by Shiyanbola et al. (2021). African American men and women with diabetes participated in focus groups centered on unearthing phenomenological, lived experiences. Within the context of these experiences, the researchers paid special attention to the role of culture in shaping beliefs about the disease. The resulting data analysis outlined key themes such as emotional representations.

In addition to interviews and focus groups, observations can be used in the qualitative strand to inform the creation of culturally specific assessments that incorporate specific contexts with an ethnographic approach (Hitchcock et al., 2005). One way to incorporate an ethnographic approach in a project with an exploratory sequential design is to consult with stakeholders about the meaning of an assessment. Multiple stakeholder input characterizes an "emic" or insider-informed inquiry to measure development.

Another use of an exploratory sequential mixed methods design is to assess the generalizability, acceptability, and feasibility of questionnaires used to measure a construct, such as psychological difficulties (Antunes et al., 2020). The study directly incorporated focus groups on therapists' feedback on using assessments with clients in the first stage. In the second stage, the feedback was sorted into themes that were used to generate a survey on the topics.

Other exploratory sequential mixed methods designs use multiple qualitative data collection methods to build a broad base of data, which is then used in designing a survey. Offering both interviews and focus groups provides ample choice for participants as they ponder whether to participate in a study and which format will feel most comfortable (Katz-Buonincontro, 2022). For example, Keshavarzian et al. (2020) used semistructured individual interviews and focus group discussions to explore reasons for smoking among adolescent Iranians. Interviews can be done in settings convenient to the participant, such as one's home rather than a clinic (Hancock et al., 2021).

Design Question: A guiding question for breaking new ground with the qualitative strand is

- Using the principle of exploration, what qualitative interview or focus group questions get to the heart of genuine experiences, perspectives, and thoughts to then build (or revise) a quantitative instrument?

Step 2: Sequence the Quantitative Strand

In this step, researchers consider how to sequence the quantitative strand in an exploratory sequential design. First, we will look at identifying qualitative themes for a quantitative instrument. Next, we will walk through ways to adapt an existing instrument.

Identifying Qualitative Themes for Development of a New Quantitative Instrument

Once the qualitative data have been collected, the data are analyzed and examined for topics that can be covered when either building a new quantitative instrument from scratch or adapting items on an existing instrument. Typically, researchers analyze themes within each interview participant and then across interview participants to make exhaustive assessments of the breadth (number) and type (quality) of potential qualitative themes. When new data are no longer needed to explain a concept, data saturation has been reached (Miles & Huberman, 1994). Synthesized literature can be used in addition to interview themes to develop survey items (de Jong et al., 2019).

Qualitative themes can be used as "domains" of a theoretical construct developed into an instrument. For example, Dehghan-nayeri et al. (2019) created 319 codes based on interviews with cardiac patients. The codes were sorted to provide the basis for an item pool that they eventually developed into a 30-item questionnaire. In another explanatory sequential mixed methods study, David et al. (2018) interviewed 12 people and identified 22 themes in their responses. They tracked the number of times each theme was mentioned within each interview and across interviews. The themes were then developed into an instrument.

It's helpful to make a concept map of the operational construct you want to measure. Concept mapping is a process for selecting the concepts to be included on an instrument (Trochim, 1989). For more guidance regarding the process of developing a brand-new instrument, you may consult resources on survey bias and sampling (Kish, 1965), survey research (Fowler, 2009), and measurement development (Wilson, 2005). Once this concept map is clarified, you can draft a set of items or statements that represent each domain.

The number of items in an instrument has a broad range—as many as 200 items or a shorter set of 30 items, for example. Each statement is rated as to its importance or priority status.

Wording and rewording statements is another critical element. Researchers can relate the statements to each other through a pile-sorting technique and then can combine them into a large matrix (Trochim, 1989). A Likert-type scale can then be created for responses to the items.

Adapting an Established Quantitative Instrument

Adapting an instrument is an iterative process. It's helpful to make a spread-sheet or table that shows an existing item; a corresponding interview quote; ways the quote differs, diverges, or expands on the item; and an adapted survey item that incorporates the interview quote (see Table 3.1). This format provides the evidence for changes to the instrument. The important question to unpack is, "How do the quotes differ, diverge, or expand on the original existing item to warrant changing or adapting the item?" In Table 3.1, an established set of scales, called the Beliefs About Creativity Scales (Hass et al., 2016), that focused on general beliefs about creativity was adapted into a new measure called Beliefs About Teaching for Creativity Scales, using quotes from teachers.

Cognitive interviews with individual respondents or very small focus groups with two or three people can be helpful for survey or instrument development. In a focus group, people can complete the adapted instrument and then air initial thoughts and feedback on it. This process helps the researcher to discern if the intent of each item is communicated well or if any items confer different meanings than originally intended. In the latter case, the researcher can further revise the wording of the item and test it again. Sometimes, it takes a few simple tweaks. Other times, a survey item can be completely restructured or even eliminated based on various statistical approaches. For example, classical test theory using factor analysis examines clusters, or sets of items, and the corresponding total score (Fan, 1998), whereas Rasch Modeling using item response theory focuses on how people respond to individual items based on item difficulty (Nunnally & Bernstein, 1994). For more information on cognitive aspects of constructing open-ended and closed-ended survey responses, see Jabine et al. (1984). Though the process may appear similar to concept mapping, adapting an instrument is not as intensive because it's not starting from scratch.

After pilot testing an adapted survey, you might add a column to your table to report the internal reliability statistic. This statistic would help you decide whether you might keep or discard the item. See David et al. (2018) for a similar table showing how mixed methods can be used to develop an instrument that measures trust.

Pilot Testing

To pilot test an adapted or new instrument, recruit a larger sample than the sample used in the first qualitative stage of the exploratory sequential mixed methods study. For example, Nunnally and Bernstein (1994) advocated for a sample size of 100, but others might suggest and approve of a smaller

TABLE 3.1. Adapting an Instrument Using Qualitative Interviews

Existing instrument item	Corresponding quote (from interview or focus group)	Ways the quote differs, diverges, or expands on the item	New or adapted survey item incorporating quote	Reliability statistic
"Talent is innate and constant throughout life." (Beliefs About Creativity Scales)	Quote (Educator A) "I like to relate it [creativity] back to a god-given talent. Like, we see people on *The Voice* or singing competitions that can sing. I feel like that's a god-given talent. Especially relating creativity to art, I would say that's a god-given talent."	New concept A: Ascribing fixed mindset about creativity as a god-given inborn talent to others, not just oneself.	"Talent is innate and constant throughout a student's life." (Adapted for Beliefs About Teaching for Creativity Scales)	Cronbach's alpha .670

Note. Data from Hass et al. (2016).

sample. In addition, ensure that the participants did not participate in pilot testing another draft of the instrument. There are many standard sampling approaches, but if you use culturally sensitive or other specialized approaches commonly used in nursing or health research, it is important to sample groups specific to a common experience, background, or other designation (such as disease classification).

Researchers aiming to ensure adequate face validity—the process of first assessing whether an instrument measures what it intends to measure—can ask experts in a specific area to review the instrument. For example, Keshavarzian et al. (2020) asked health experts to review the Cigarette Smoking Obscenity Scale they developed based on interviews and focus groups with Iranian adolescents. How many experts you consult depends on the access to experts and the diversity of the expert pool; you want to ensure it adequately represents the various points of view on the topic. For example, consider your primary stakeholders. Depending on the field, stakeholders might be health professionals, education professionals, religious officials, parents, or other community members who have deep knowledge on the topic. Data analysis of a newly piloted or adapted instrument would use factor analysis or item response theory, for example.

Design Questions: Guiding questions for developing the quantitative strand in an exploratory sequential mixed methods study include

- Does the quantitative instrument, measure, or survey adequately span the themes elicited from the qualitative data?
- What does the piloting process and resulting pilot data tell you about the survey or instrument?
- Do I need to consult with stakeholders and disciplinary experts?

Step 3: Compare Qualitative and Quantitative Results

As with explanatory designs, exploratory designs include the important final step of comparing the qualitative and quantitative results. In particular, the comparison would examine whether the qualitative interviews or focus groups (Step 1: Qualitative strand) provided new themes for forming a new instrument or adapting an existing instrument (Step 2: Quantitative strand). For example, in an exploratory sequential mixed methods study, Cabrera (2011) interviewed college students about the racial diversity of collegiate friendships. They coded the interviews using pattern matching (Yin, 2008) in four frames of color-blind racism ideology and developed the interview themes into a longitudinal survey administered to a larger group of college students. They then used analysis of variance (ANOVA) to examine mean differences across four student groups and Scheffe's post-hoc tests to examine these differences in more detail, as well as regression analysis to predict first-year students' racial ideologies.

Some researchers choose to continue collecting qualitative data after a new survey is piloted. The purpose of gathering additional data is to examine any discrepancies. For example, Bacon (2020) used autobiographies to form a survey and then formed focus groups and reflection essays to better understand linguistically responsive teaching practices.

Other researchers examine construct validity using the statistical technique of exploratory factor analysis (EFA). Construct validity takes face validity beyond expert opinions about which concepts are essential. EFA tests whether the concepts are indeed measurable. The purpose of using EFA is to see whether survey items clusters into factors and, if so, whether those factors align conceptually with the original intention of the survey as developed through the interviews and/or focus group themes. Other ways to examine measurement properties of a new survey are confirmatory factor analysis, Cronbach's alpha (to test for internal reliability), and other statistics to assess predictive validity. Internal reliability is computed statistically using. Predictive validity is examined by testing whether actual real human behaviors can be forecasted based on how the survey is filled out. Other exploratory sequential data analyses might aim to compare subgroups along various dependent variables such as care preferences, for example (de Jong et al., 2019).

Design Questions: Guiding questions for comparing the qualitative results with the quantitative results in an exploratory sequential mixed methods study include

• How did the qualitative results inform the quantitative results?
• Are there additional ways to analyze the data?

SUMMARY

Chapter 3 presented two frequently used mixed methods designs in psychological, educational, health and medical research: explanatory sequential and exploratory sequential mixed methods designs. Common to both designs is the clear and strategic use of stages that work in tandem. Like a tandem bicycle that depends on both bicyclists, the quantitative and qualitative data are designed in consideration of each other. Instead of existing in isolation, each data set can help clarify, strengthen, and improve the quality of the other data set for a greater common methodological purpose. Both explanatory and exploratory designs balance the philosophical principles of humanism—understanding the diverse breadth of people and their experiences—and pragmatism—helping people with applied science. These designs are popular because they provide rigorous ways to study people, explicitly including and amplifying their voices without compromising scientific methods to measure behaviors, experiences, perspectives, and beliefs. Chapter 4 includes discussion of convergent (or concurrent) mixed methods designs that do not use separate sequential stages but rather collect quantitative and qualitative data simultaneously.

4 CONVERGENT MIXED METHODS DESIGNS

If sequential mixed methods designs are like a tandem bicycle, then convergent designs are like a twin set of mirrors reflecting light off each other. The concept of reciprocal illumination (Myers et al., 2020) offers an especially useful way to think about the convergent relationship between qualitative and quantitative data as each shine light on the interpretation of the results.

Convergent or concurrent mixed methods (also called "parallel") projects gather quantitative and qualitative data separately, or parallel to each other. In convergent designs, unlike in sequential mixed methods designs, the data design, collection, and analysis do not influence a later stage of data collection. Instead, quantitative and qualitative data are independently collected but coexist in the same study. How, then, do we prevent a convergent mixed methods study from becoming a "kitchen sink" approach to research, in which multiple types of data are collected together without a clear intent? The challenge with convergent mixed methods designs is that they seem rather easy to pull off in the beginning, but they can be a little tricky to analyze near the end of the project, for two reasons. First, the data are not purposefully linked at the sampling stage. Second, because data are not linked, the design of the

https://doi.org/10.1037/0000404-005
How to Mix Methods: A Guide to Sequential, Convergent, and Experimental Research Designs, by J. Katz-Buonincontro

quantitative measure or qualitative protocol is not influenced by data analysis from a prior stage.

These issues raise the question of how to analyze data separately and then merge the data. In the final merging stage, the results can be confirmed, challenged, or otherwise discussed. Convergent designs were first called "concurrent" to accentuate the mutual timing of data collection, but the name of the design has recently been changed to "convergent" to emphasize the importance of merging the data sets (Creswell, 2022).

> Chapter 4 explains the steps used in convergent mixed methods designs in which quantitative and qualitative data are gathered separately within a relatively close time frame. The data are analyzed separately and then compared, or merged, at the end of the project. Exemplar studies are provided to give you a sense of the ways that researchers design and approach the challenge of converging data sets.

STEPS

Figure 4.1 shows the basic steps in designing a convergent mixed methods project. As discussed in Chapter 3, allow for flexibility in the design of the project instead of following the steps in a rigid manner. You'll likely adjust different aspects, such as when and how to collect the data in a convergent project.

Mixed methods researcher Dr. Jean Providence Nzabonimpa, Head of the Regional Evaluation Unit with the United Nations World Food Programme, described her use of convergent or parallel mixed methods designs as follows:

> When I started the doctoral journey into social science methodologies, I was intrigued by the mixing of qualitative and quantitative data, wondering whether qualitative and quantitative results would be the same in a convergent parallel mixed methods design. My first assumption was that such convergence of results might not be achievable. I further reflected on what would happen in a second phase with participants in the qualitative methods-strand switching data collection tools with survey respondents. With a control group built in the design, I ended up with a "convergent cross-over mixed methods design and analysis," which allowed me to assess whether similar data are gathered, and results produced, regardless of once-off participation (control group) or

FIGURE 4.1. Design Steps for Convergent Mixed Methods

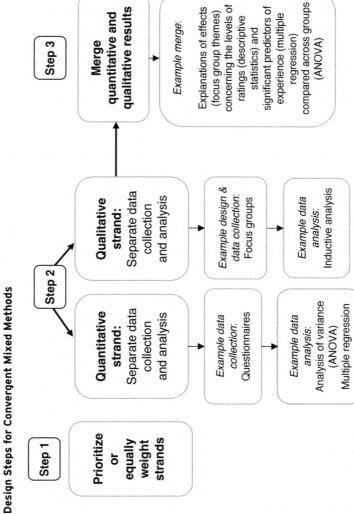

two-times participation in the experimental group. There were merits and demerits of convergent designs, but results were illuminated with the crossover design. There are mixed results with larger effect sizes observed in phase one than in phase two, and vice versa. The equal-priority claims in convergent designs do not necessarily ensure equality between the methods strands. The take-home lesson is that without conducting the analysis in an iterative and looping manner, navigating back and forth between narrative and numerical data, the qualitative data become de-contextualized through quantitizing, while the quantitative data are fleshed out with insights generated through the researcher's interpretation. (personal communication, September 7, 2023)

Notice how Dr. Nzabonimpa wrestled with making sense of the data, without stopping with her first approach.

Let's look further into how to emphasize or weight the strands of a mixed methods project in the next sections.

Step 1: Prioritizing or Equally Weighting the Quantitative and Qualitative Strands

Convergent designs might not necessarily have an obvious starting point the way that sequential designs do. So, how do we prioritize or emphasize the importance of either or both the quantitative and qualitative data in a convergent design? Although some researchers argue it is not necessary to contemplate the prioritization of data (Creswell, 2022), it's often natural to give preference to one data set. That's why it's worth contemplating how to weight them.

The emphasis is generally noted by capitalizing the method that is prioritized, or emphasized, such as QUAN + qual or QUAL + quan. The capitalization signals whether the quantitative research questions and hypotheses are posed first and emphasized or the qualitative research questions are posed first and consequently emphasized as a main thrust of the project. For convergent designs that weight both data equally, no capitalization is necessary. If you do not want to prioritize either type of data, you may opt not to capitalize the notated method, as in qual + quan or quan + qual. To note, it is not mandatory to include the notation in a publication.

Most often, the quantitative and qualitative data collection occur in the same timeframe. But they don't necessarily occur at the exact same time. Ideally, the qualitative data is generated from the sample used for the quantitative data (Creswell, 2022), although some researchers don't feel that's necessary. For example, researchers may administer a student survey using specific criteria to select the sample and may select a sample of students for interviews who meet the same criteria, without knowing whether the second sample includes students who filled out the survey (White et al., 2019). In this way, one sample might have some participants taking the survey and some participants participating in the interview, but that's pretty atypical. Usually, researchers track the participants so they know who participates in the quantitative data collection and who participates in the qualitative data collection. If it is important for participants to participate in both the quantitative and qualitative strands of the convergent project, it is especially important to track the completion of participation in each part of the project.

Sampling presents a challenge with convergent mixed methods projects. In published convergent mixed methods studies, it's not always clear or obvious how each wave of participants is sampled. For example, in one equally weighted convergent mixed methods project (Myers et al., 2020), qualitative interviews were first performed with six randomly selected teacher education students. Written reflections were also gathered from these students. Two quantitative observations were conducted of the teacher education students' teaching performance, but it was not clear how those two classroom sessions were selected from all the classroom sessions in the teacher education students' practicum course. In addition, quantitative teacher mathematical knowledge assessment data were collected. When multiple data sources are used, it's important to tell the reader which participants participate in each activity to avoid ambiguity in sampling and which subjects participate in data collection.

Design Questions: To begin Step 1, think about the 10 essential design features of mixed methods research introduced in Chapter 2. Consider the weighting of the quantitative and qualitative data:

- Which data will I prioritize, or will the data be equally weighted?
- As a result of either prioritization or equal weighting, how will I order the qualitative and quantitative research questions and hypotheses?

Step 2: Capturing Co-Occurrence Through Data Collection

A specific site, program, or case in which multiple activities occur lends itself well to the concurrent mixed methods design because the researcher does not have to orchestrate the timing of the events. Rather, the researcher seeks to capture the co-occurring nature of participation. Examples of such sites include a school (Wilson et al., 2022), a class (Zhang et al., 2022), or a specific type of treatment (Cyr et al., 2022). As Cyr et al. expressed, lived experiences such as coping and recovery can have nonlinear trajectories. Hence, co-occurring events and nonlinear trajectories are fitting for convergent mixed methods designs.

A decision to study multiple events implies ample opportunities to collect data over time. For example, student engagement data can be measured quantitatively in several different ways. It's helpful to think about the number of activities that will yield useful data. That is, if you are studying student engagement with a convergent mixed methods design, you could look at student engagement in the classroom, in study sessions, in applied settings, or during independent work time.

In addition to deciding the activities to focus on, consider how many points in time you plan to collect data, such as capitalizing on the start of a new activity or session. Attention to start dates of planned activities allows the researcher to calibrate engagement of participants in these special activities or sessions.

Lastly, the instrument or protocol to use or develop for data collection must capture engagement in the activities in focus. Selection of instruments should be designed to align well to those tasks: How do the quantitative or qualitative data represent authentic engagement in the activities? For example, self-report surveys can capture opinions and perspectives on a specific activity. Observations focus more on the interactions among people and their expressed behavior. Interviews concentrate on individual perspectives. Focus groups can be suitable for book-ending an experience with group discussions. Drawings or other artistic representations provide a reflective component of experience after it happens.

Design Questions: For Step 2, think about what would make your mixed methods project truly convergent, as opposed to sequential:

- What co-occurring or nonlinear trajectories will you seek to capture in your convergent mixed methods project?

- What naturally occurring events might you capitalize on with a convergent design?

- For the sample, will the participants participate in both the qualitative and quantitative strands of data collection?

Step 3: Merging Qualitative and Quantitative Results

As mentioned in the introduction to this chapter, reciprocal illumination refers to the convergent merging process. One way to further unpack the merging process, when quantitative data collection comes first, is to think of a quantitative marker or set of markers illuminated with qualitative explanations. When the researcher collects qualitative data first, the merging of results can be conceptualized as highlighting a qualitative experience with quantitative indicators of change over time.

The merging process can highlight similarities or bear discordance. For example, Cyr et al. (2022) noted that participants' qualitative characterizations of posttraumatic stress disorder recovery differed from their quantitative symptom scores. The authors attributed the difference to the dynamic aspect of this posttraumatic stress recovery, which harkens back to the nonlinear trajectories. The discordance also points to the different stages of recovery that participants might be in.

In addition to finding out why the qualitative and quantitative data may differ or even contradict each other, the convergent merging process can highlight differences between or among subgroups in the sample. For example, Mehra et al. (2021) compared youth who had or had not sought psychotherapy, finding that the youth who had experienced psychotherapy reported greater readiness to change and received encouragement to do so.

Students can provide their own unique identifiers when responding to a survey and use that same unique identifier when signing up for an interview or focus group. The unique identifier provides a link across the quantitative and qualitative data. Students can email their instructor proof of completion if extra credit is provided, and this proof can be automatically generated from electronic surveys without revealing their unique identifier.

Some convergent studies use a single survey to collect both closed-ended and open-ended responses. Open-ended responses or free text response-writing allows for understanding a critical process, especially when meeting face to face is not an option because of geographical disparities or health-related issues like the COVID-19 pandemic (Choi et al., 2022). Although open-ended responses can be valuable, one note of caution is that participants can copy and paste responses from external sources while filling out the survey (Lacy et al., 2021). So as not to jeopardize the validity of responses, it can be helpful to make the free-response prompts very specific, with a notation as to the length of response.

As an example, McDonnell et al. (2022) conducted a convergent mixed methods study to understand the experience of managing waiting lists during the COVID-19 pandemic from the perspective of psychologists. The quantitative data provided an overview of the literal, practical, administrative burdens while the qualitative data provided a sense of the emotional burdens and perceived stress levels of the psychologists. This example reflects the need to get a deeper understanding of quantitative data (Lacy et al., 2021) by unearthing reasons, causes, and consequences of a phenomenon via qualitative data (Fentaw et al., 2022).

Data Transformation Approach

The data transformation approach is considered a convergent mixed methods design. Both quantitative and qualitative analyses can be performed with one set of raw data. In this way, one data set is interpreted in two complimentary ways (Morse, 1991). Using one data set, the researcher starts with either the quantitative or the qualitative task and transforms it. Mixed methods researchers use the terms "quantitizing" and "qualitizing" to describe the transformation process.

Quantitizing refers to the process in which codes (are) attached to segments of text and numerical values (are) then assigned to those codes (Sandelowski et al., 2009). There are several quantitizing approaches. For example, frequencies of codes can denote how many times something occurs but cannot be statistically analyzed beyond descriptive statistics. Bergman (2010) argued for a presence–absence dichotomous coding scheme (0 = *no presence*, 1 = *presence*). In addition to frequency counts and dichotomous coding, the salience or strength can be examined using ordinal data as expressed by a Likert-type scale (0 = *no evidence*, 1 = *minimal evidence*, 2 = *moderate evidence*, 3 = *strong evidence*). Another term for this coding process is "intensity coding" (Strauss & Corbin, 1994). An example statistical comparison of the means across the groups can be made using the Kruskall-Wallis test, for example, which is a nonparametric way of testing two or more independent samples of equal or different sample sizes.

When coding qualitatively, researchers can transform quantitative data into qualitative data, similar to the process of factor analysis, which relies on naming clusters of variables. According to Nzabonimpa (2018), qualitizing means "finding or imposing an underlying conceptual qualitative representation of the items that make up the factor or the denominator concept which is shared among the items loading together" (p. 3). For example, video recordings of naturalistic behavior such as classroom teaching can be transcribed and coded qualitatively. The same set of videos can also be coded quantitatively to examine the presence, frequency, and salience (or strength) of certain behaviors. The next sections explore further what this might mean.

Qualitative Coding

Sometimes representing human thought and behavior with numbers and words does not suffice. Videos are a great tool for capturing multimodal expression, which includes body language or gestures, oral expression, and social interactions (Katz-Buonincontro et al., 2020). Multimodal expression refers to simultaneous or co-occurring expressions of behavior, such as talking and dancing at the same time.

Videos can be watched, transcribed, and viewed multiple times for data analysis purposes. A focus on only one type of expression might not do justice to a specific behavior, and so analyzing multiple modes of expression might be fitting. As such, the qualitative coding of videos helps to ensure that a full range of expression is noticed and included. Coding is typically segmented to the smallest conceptual unit (Lincoln & Guba, 1985) while making sure each code is mutually exclusive (Merriam, 2009). The smallest conceptual unit generally refers to a concept that cannot further be broken down. For example, a research project on friendship might break down codes to specific, discrete examples of friendship bonds, such as sharing emotional experiences, advice, resources, time, money, and so on. For further examples of qualitative coding approaches, see Katz-Buonincontro (2022) as well as other qualitative research textbooks.

Quantitative Coding

Once the qualitative codes are established, they can be compared across specific groups (such as classrooms or organizational units) or instances (such as days or weeks). For example, the frequency, presence, or salience of the codes can be established. Historically, techniques like quantitative content analysis have been used to count words, phrases, or images and then apply statistical analyses (Bergman, 2010).

Design Questions: For Step 3, merging qualitative and quantitative data analyses, think about how you will converge, or merge, the data that are most meaningful to the original research purpose:

- Considering the principle of reciprocal illumination, how do the quantitative and qualitative results compare to each other?
- What are some possible explanations for this relationship?

SUMMARY

Chapter 4 reviews convergent designs, initially called "concurrent" or "parallel" designs, to emphasize the co-occurrence of qualitative and quantitative data collection, in contrast to sequential designs in which data collected in a primary stage influence a subsequent stage of data collection. Convergent designs work well with co-occurring or nonlinear trajectories of learning, treatment, and other real-life experiences. To refrain from a "kitchen sink" or possibly haphazard or unclear arrangement of data collection and analysis, researchers try to match the data as closely as possible to the authentic experiences of the participants using the principle of representativeness. That is, the measure or protocol should represent authentic behaviors or thought processes. In a convergent design, although the data are frequently collected independent of each other, the results are merged or compared at the end, hence highlighting the effort to bring the quantitative and qualitative together for reciprocal illumination. Chapter 5 introduces experimental mixed methods designs that develop and test a planned intervention.

5 EXPERIMENTAL MIXED METHODS DESIGNS

Mixed methods designs that include an experiment or a quasi-experiment are probably the most advanced skill-wise and are the most resource intensive. That's because the "special sauce" in mixed methods experiments is the cleverness of the actual design using rigorous controls, the availability of necessary lab space and equipment, and the appropriate coupling of qualitative data (typically from interviews) that relate to the constructs under examination in a valid way. Quasi-experiments also require rigorous design but use random assignment of groups rather than random assignment of individual participants to treatments. Because experiments test detectable differences in treatments or conditions, they are not a hallmark of all social sciences. Therefore, the design has been, to this point, most extensively used among psychology, health, and medical researchers and students, and it has been used to a lesser extent in education and arts research. If you are new to experimental research, consider working with a trained experimenter at first, but do not let your inexperience discourage your imagination when designing your mixed methods research project!

https://doi.org/10.1037/0000404-006
How to Mix Methods: A Guide to Sequential, Convergent, and Experimental Research Designs, by J. Katz-Buonincontro

Four types of experimental mixed methods designs are covered in this chapter: basic designs, case studies generated from experiments, art and arts-based therapy intervention designs, and designs using physiological measures. At the heart of experimental mixed methods projects lies a carefully planned and designed intervention. As such, experimental mixed methods designs are markedly different and arguably more time intensive than other mixed methods designs. The closest "sister" to mixed methods design is the sequential explanatory design. The staging of quantitative intervention data collection followed by qualitative data collection to garner feedback on the intervention resembles the way in which a quantitative survey coupled with explanatory interviews would be run (sequential mixed methods). A less common design places interviews before or during the experiment, or both. This chapter includes three ways (before, during, after) of using qualitative methods combined with interventions.

Chapter 5 reviews four experimental mixed methods designs in which the quantitative strand is prioritized as the main part of the study: basic, case study, arts-based, and physiological. Exemplar studies in various fields such as psychology, medicine, and creative art therapy offer a sense of the ways in which researchers design interventions in unique ways under the umbrella design of experimental mixed methods. Tables contrast experimental and quasi-experimental features and explain the four types of experimental mixed-methods designs. A figure clearly labels the elements of the design to guide you through the options.

OVERVIEW

In the mixed methods literature, you might find different ways of describing experimental designs. Some scholars call them "complex designs" (Creswell, 2022), and some authors do not use the term "experiment" in the title of a mixed methods research article, even though an intervention is used (e.g., Parke et al., 2021; Rogers et al., 2019). Some experiments combined with interviews are referred to as sequential designs (e.g., Li & Xu, 2019). Because of this variation, it can be a little tricky to find articles that serve as exemplars for the experimental mixed methods design you might want to model your project after. As researchers recognize the importance of using culturally specific approaches in research (discussed more in depth later in this chapter), qualitative components of experimental work are becoming more acceptable so that interventions are tailored to the needs and concerns of various communities.

What do researchers need to know to run an experiment? This section briefly introduces and compares experimental to quasi-experimental research as used in a mixed methods project. A basic overview of key concepts and terms related to conducting an experimental mixed methods design is included to help you prepare and design your project. For additional details on the development of the theory and application of experimental research, measurement, and assessment, you may want to consult books on experiments (e.g., Shadish et al., 2002), classical test theory and item response theory (Nunnally & Bernstein, 1994), and survey development (Dillman, 2000).

Experimental Research

Understanding cause and effect is the essence of science. Experiments focus on isolating and examining a narrow representation of how things work to develop microcosmic understandings (MacLin, 2020). Experimental research is the sine qua non of psychological science. It's also used in other related fields, including education, medicine, and health. The purpose of experiments is to examine the effects of an activity, treatment, medicine, or other type of planned intervention.

Why is experimental research important? Intervention effects can help explain key processes and may provide a comparative understanding of ways to modify behavior or improve health, well-being, and disease, to name but a few areas. Following are some basic features of experimental research to consider when designing an experimental mixed methods study. You may want to consult core textbooks in experimental psychology to understand the nuances of experiments and to select an experimental design appropriate for your research area.

Manipulated Variable and Measures

Experimenters introduce an independent or manipulated variable. The dependent variable changes, or varies, based on the independent variable. In addition, experimenters can select subject variables, which can be demographic categories such as gender or race, personality types, thinking patterns, or other types of performance measures.

Experimenters test hypotheses regarding the relationship of these variables using inferential statistics. How do we decide which variables to test, and which measures to use? Researchers may select measures based on past literature. To start, scour the databases for measures related to the constructs that will be evaluated in the intervention. You can make a list of relevant measures and decide how many to include in the study. For example, Kim and Lim (2013) ran a quasi-experimental mixed methods study of mathematics learning. Instead of just testing mathematics attitudes (math likeability), they also tested mathematics self-efficacy (belief in math learnability). They could have also measured math anxiety, for example. It's your choice to make similar distinctions. Keep your experimental design narrow, focused, and clear.

For mixed methods experimental projects, another way to select measures is based on preliminary qualitative interviews with a group of participants in the field who have experiential knowledge on the intervention topic. For example, Bennett et al. (2020) selected the Fatigue-Inertia subscale of the Profile of Mood States (McNair et al., 1971) measure to use in the experiment because interviewees noted during interviews the importance of energy and attention. In that study, the researchers relied on qualitative input from participants to help guide and select the measures and variables for the experimental component of the mixed measures study.

Baseline Data Collection

Many experiments involve collection of baseline data or psychological characteristics from the participants prior to the intervention, commonly referred to as "A" in experimenter parlance. Baseline data allow for statistical comparison of measured changes, rates, or performances before and after an intervention. In ABA designs, a target behavior is first observed ("A"), then the independent variable or treatment is introduced ("B"), and then the variable is removed to ascertain the effects on "A" (MacLin, 2020). Additional experimental variables can also be introduced, extending this design to AB1, AB2A, AB1AB2AB3A, for example.

Random Assignment and Random Sampling

Another key principle for designing experiments is the random assignment of participants to treatments. In between-subjects designs, participants are randomly assigned to either the experimental/treatment or the control group. Some mixed methods experimental projects have multiple treatment/experimental conditions. Typically, researchers find gaps in the literature that indicate what has not been tested, which helps to determine the type and number of treatment groups necessary to fill that gap.

If possible, conduct random sampling before assigning participants to different conditions, treatments, or interventions (Shadish et al., 2002). The reason is that the average causal relationship observed in the sample assigned to that condition would then be the same as that observed from the population from which the sample is derived. Settings for conducting experiments can also be randomly sampled (e.g., hospitals, schools, clinics), although this sampling method is not used frequently in these settings because it can be hard to do.

Intervention and Control Groups

Planned interventions are the purposeful design of a specific treatment or intervention or set of interventions to administer in the experiment. Between-subjects designs examine the effects of a treatment/condition across two or more groups (at least one treatment group and a control group, in which the treatment is absent). Within-subjects designs examine two or more treatments/conditions within each participant. In within-subjects designs, the participants act as their own controls; the design does not include separate treatment and control conditions. Some disadvantages of this design are that the effects of the treatment might influence any subsequent treatment and that the participant might change their response based on learning the goal of the experiment (MacLin, 2020).

Experimental Setup and Stimuli

Planning the experimental setup and stimuli involves designing the intervention steps and thinking about how the interventions differ. Outlining and diagramming the physical setup is a good place to start. That way you can discuss how to make sure you have the necessary equipment and facilities to adequately run the experiments. Piloting the experiment ensures that the study participants are comfortable both physically and psychologically.

Field-based experiments integrate an intervention into macrocosmic or real-life situations, as opposed to studying microcosmic or laboratory-based observations (MacLin, 2020). Developed initially by psychologists in the 1960s (Campbell & Stanley, 1966), this type of research is important for studying behaviors when it is not possible to use a laboratory or when the behavior occurs only in a naturalistic setting. Examples of naturalistic settings are classrooms, daycare centers, clinics, hospitals, outpatient centers, art studios, and therapy offices.

Quasi-Experimental Research

Quasi-experimental research lacks random assignment to conditions and does not necessarily include control conditions. A pretest–posttest design or a posttest-only design can be used (see Shadish et al., 2002). Sometimes, the strategy of matching is used to group sites or groups with similar characteristics when the researchers anticipate that these characteristics will significantly predict the dependent variable. In this book, I abbreviate ways to match or stratify groups, and you can read more deeply about these techniques in other resources.

A challenge to using quasi-experimental designs is the open-ended nature of a setting in which variables cannot be controlled (e.g., as a result of environmental variables or unanticipated events). However, variables can be introduced, such as a type of treatment, instruction, activity, or therapy. For explanation of threats to validity, please refer to a research or statistics textbook.

It is most likely not possible to randomly assign groups to an intervention in a quasi-experimental phase of a mixed methods design, but it is possible to use counterbalanced designs. Counterbalanced designs provide a treatment/intervention to all groups but in different orders. The tricky thing about this design is that an earlier treatment might affect a later treatment. It is possible, though, to statistically separate the effects of the treatment from the order of the treatment.

In addition to counterbalanced designs, time-series designs can be used in quasi-experimental research, wherein an intervention is used with an intact group, as opposed to random assignment and random sampling. Time-series designs include multiple pretests with a group to assess the stability of pretest scores and multiple posttests to assess change attributable to the intervention. Table 5.1 compares characteristics of experiments and quasi-experiments.

FOUR EXPERIMENTAL MIXED METHODS DESIGNS

As covered so far in this book, mixed methods designs are developed as a result of many needs and interests. One prominent interest is the drive to make social and scientific progress through purposefully addressing historical biases in quantitative methodology using White, educated, industrialized, rich, and democratic (WEIRD) samples (American Psychological Association, 2020) through the adaptation of psychological measures to the lived experiences of diverse communities. In addition to compensating for such scientific distortions and omissions (Dattilio et al., 2010), mixed methodologists use their creativity to combine data in innovative ways that capitalize on human expression. To demonstrate these two issues of cultural responsiveness and human creative expression, this section presents unique ways that

TABLE 5.1. Comparison of Experiments and Quasi-Experiments

Dimension	Experiment	Quasi-experiment
Focus on causation	Manipulation of treatment to occur before the effect	Manipulation of treatment to occur before the effect
Construction of reality	Microcosmic	Macrocosmic
Setting	Laboratory	Natural life (e.g., classroom, hospital)
Design considerations	Quality of facilities, equipment, and personnel	Boundary of the experiment and possible naturalistic considerations or unintended interferences
Sampling choices	Purposive or convenient sampling of participants	Intact, purposive, or convenient sampling of participants
	Random assignment of participants to conditions	No random assignment to conditions but counter-balanced designs may be possible
	Random sampling of participants	Random selection of naturalistic sites for multisite experiments
		Purposive or convenient selection of naturalistic sites

researchers continue to develop and adapt experimental mixed methods designs to better address the needs and lived realities of people, including clients, patients, students, community members. Table 5.2 and the following sections present the four most common types of experimental mixed methods designs.

Basic Experimental or Quasi-Experimental Mixed Methods Design

This type of design is the most common, with a conventional experiment either in the lab or in a naturalistic setting such as a workplace, classroom, or community setting typically combined with a relatively brief interview placed before, during, or after the experiment. Though other types of qualitative data collection methods, such as focus groups or observations, can be paired with interventions in a mixed methods design, interviews are the most prevalent choice for pairing with an intervention.

Why conduct a mixed methods experiment, as opposed to a regular experiment? Experimental mixed methods designs characteristically include just one experiment, whereas regular experimental research might include one or more experiments, which are then reported together in a journal article.

TABLE 5.2. Types of Experimental Mixed Methods Designs

Type of design	Quantitative method	Qualitative method	Special features and considerations
Basic experiment or quasi-experiment	Experiment or intervention	Interviews before, during, or after intervention	Experimental or quasi-experimental
Case study	Multiple points of case measurement (e.g., the beginning, middle, and end of a treatment)	Use of thorough or "thick" description of cases	Careful selection of cases from a larger experiment
Arts or arts therapy	Arts-based intervention or curriculum	Interviews about making art and/or observation of the arts activities	Well-developed art therapy or art activity
Physiological data	Comparison of physiological measure to self-report and objective measures	Think aloud procedures or postintervention exit interviews about brain states or emotional experiences	Pattern-matching phenomenological interview descriptions; inclusion of data on physiological or neural configurations

Instead of trying to test a hypothesis with several experiments, researchers using mixed methods experimental designs can go deeper into the experience of the participants and therefore can take more time to run an experiment and to analyze data, and they can require more time from the participants (and hence potentially more compensation or extra credit). Therefore, mixed methods experimental designs require an open-minded, multipronged inquiry approach in which experimental results alone do not suffice to answer the research question. Mixed methods experimental researchers often straddle both research and practice—they don't want to give up one to privilege the other. Thus, they value more than simple feedback ratings from participants on their intervention experiences—they value their explanations, experiences, and perspectives. That's why four exciting types of mixed methods experiments are discussed in this chapter.

Case Study

This type of mixed methods experimental design helps provide a level of detailed scrutiny of individual study participants. In certain fields, concern has been growing about the proper selection of treatments to include in experimental research as well as the quality of the conclusions that can be derived from experimental research and then incorporated into practice. In turn, these concerns have driven professionals to look for new ways to understand the causes, antecedents, and experiences of study participants (Dattilio et al., 2010). In some fields, such as psychotherapy, for instance, it can be beneficial to magnify and take a closer look at individual results within the wider sample of those who have participated in a random control trial. That means selecting and comparing people, classrooms, or sites.

Researchers conducting case studies select and compare units that have similar properties or parallel boundaries (Yin, 2008). The selection criteria for examining cases from larger experimental studies might be based on outlier or extreme differences in scores, or clients who have poor outcomes or do not respond to a treatment (Dattilio et al., 2010).

Single case study experiments may be limited in generalizability but can provide a strong and clear picture of a microcosm of life unique to a certain individual who might have certain diagnoses. In these situations, researchers consider how to dig deeper into data to carefully sample cases for further analyses. Mixed methods researchers can pull individual cases from a larger quantitative data set to analyze in a focused way (Teddlie & Yu, 2007). The objective when sampling cases from a larger data set can be to provide a complimentary representativeness in terms of balancing breadth (larger data set) with depth (smaller, focused data set). The smaller data set can be either quantitative or qualitative. The most important decision in mixed methods case sampling is the reason for selecting the smaller data set, to ensure that the smaller data set answers the research question and relates to the larger set.

In informal practice among psychotherapists or teachers, for example, it can be common to think about different ways people react to certain types of treatment or instruction. Case study methodology more formally addresses individual differences using quantitative data (e.g., changes in levels of a psychological state over time) coupled with individualized narratives detailing a participant's history. As a result, the researcher can compare different outcome trajectories (Dattilio et al., 2010).

Researchers interested in taking action based on case study research can apply lessons learned to future interventions or instruction, especially in schools and other community-based decision-making organizations (see Mertler, 2012; Sagor, 2005; Stringer, 2007). In epidemiology, cases may be used in yet another way. For example, patient cases can be generated based on disease and health history. Retrospective data may then be collected to examine the history of the patient. These studies are called case-control experiments (Shadish et al., 2002).

Arts-Based and Arts Therapy

Artistic development and therapeutic treatment in the arts (music, dance, theatre, visual arts, spoken word) compel researchers to pioneer new experimental mixed methods approaches. When skillfully planned, the researcher can engage a study participant in an art activity to access thoughts, feelings, or needs that may not be easily accessible through speaking or writing (Keegan, 2008). Distant memories or undesired experiences are examples of hard-to-access thoughts and feelings. The reason perspectives may not be easily accessible is that they may be challenging to verbalize, for example because of a child's developmental stage, or they may be hard to verbalize and express publicly, difficult to remember, or difficult to describe through words alone. Psychodynamics of these thoughts can be teased out through images (Gieser & Stein, 1999).

Researchers use arts approaches in medical or therapeutic settings to examine their effects on patients and clients. In these studies, consenting patients are randomly assigned to participate in different types of art to help treat illness or anxiety. Music therapy, for example, includes activities to address stress and anxiety associated with a particular disease or form of trauma. In one music therapy study, 31 adult cancer patients engaged in music activities for the purpose of addressing trauma in a hospital (Bradt et al., 2015). The researchers used quantitative instruments to indicate the degree to which the people (as a group) experienced mood anxiety, and the qualitative interview protocols were used to engage participants, individually, about the intervention experience once it was over. In another example, a quasi-experimental mixed methods study using the arts, Keown (2013) interleaved quantitative data collection with three types of qualitative data (analysis of art created in a project, observations, interviews). Multiple sources of data were used to triangulate the arts-based curriculum supporting leadership development in adolescent girls, who took a leadership self-efficacy scale before and after the curriculum.

Reporting arts-based experimental mixed methods studies requires some unique considerations. When presenting the findings of these studies, researchers should provide adequate detail about the art activity (e.g., the steps and setting of a drawing activity), the art experience (e.g., type of theatre production and any relevant setup or setting), or the art therapy technique (e.g., music therapy sessions). These descriptions help the audience understand not only what type of art activity occurred but also the guiding concept, purpose, or educational/treatment theory behind the art activity. Additionally, because the arts use multimodal forms of expression, it is helpful to provide supporting documentation such as hand-drawn maps, photographs, videos, or audio recordings of participants making the art so the visual qualities and sounds can help represent the activities in multiple dimensions. Also, note that reserving some or all of the arts activities helps with the data analysis process because the researcher can review the arts activities and notice details that may have initially seemed insignificant. When using the arts, consider obtaining consent from participants for such recordings in addition to qualitative and quantitative data collection.

Finally, it is important to describe if and how the members of the research team interacted with professional artists, art teachers, or art therapists, for example, to provide the art activity. This shows self-reflexivity on the part of the researcher and clarifies potential threats to validity such as halo/social desirability effects.

Anticipating the meaning of artistic expression can provide counter-intuitive results. In one mixed methods study, Hume et al. (2005) studied 10-year-old children's ($n = 147$) hand-drawn maps of their homes and neighborhoods for instances of physical activity. The children's physical activity was measured with accelerometers, which measure motion, and the data were analyzed using t tests (examining the means across groups) and linear regression analyses (examining the relationships among independent and dependent variables). Boys who drew more opportunities for sedentary activity in their homes were actually more likely than others to engage in vigorous activity outdoors, $F(1, 60) = 4.06$, $p < .05$, and they spent less time being sedentary.

Compared to verbal and numerical data, arts-based data can provide a deep focus on individual participants and how they make meaning out of what is being asked of them in a research study. Dr. Mandy Archibald, an interdisciplinary artist serving as a professor in the College of Nursing in the Rady Faculty of Health Sciences at the University of Manitoba, described her engagement with arts-based mixed methods research:

> I first started doing mixed methods research to understand and position diverse knowledge sources in dialogue with one another. The need for this dialogical approach arose initially during my graduate training when I was confronted with a tension between individuals' experiences of illness and the empirical knowledge around treatment and medical management. At that time, I became interested in how the arts could become a place to integrate these diverse sources and representations of knowledge, recognizing that since our experiences of the world are in fact holistic, such resources would also benefit from integrating diverse understandings. What culminated as a tangible knowledge resource for families also inspired further empirical and theoretical work into how the arts and mixed methods relate, how they can be integrated, in which forms, with which considerations, and to what benefit.

At this time, there was no writing on the integration of arts and specifically arts-based research methodology within mixed methods models. Moving forward, I conducted a number of studies that helped to advance my understanding of the relationship between arts and mixed methods research. For example, as part of a transdisciplinary centre of research excellence, I conducted a series of arts elicitation focus groups with 39 older adults in South Australia, to better understand their experiences of frailty and perceptions of frailty screening. The arts-based data provided new insights into the unspeakable aspects of frailty that reflected loss of identity. (personal communication, May 5, 2023)

Inclusion of Physiological Data

An emergent area of experimental mixed methods research is the inclusion of physiological or biological specimens. The reason for considering inclusion of these factors is that researchers are increasingly interested with how the body responds to different scenarios. Additionally, researchers are concerned with the validity of responses on quantitative self-report measures. The addition of physiological measures can provide a relatively stable source of evidence; physiological responses can tell us many different things about emotions, stress indicators elicited under various experimental conditions, and the ways in which these responses affect certain cognitive outcomes. For example, the autonomic nervous system can produce reactions such as heart rate, cardiac output, ventricle contractility, and peripheral resistance (Akinola et al., 2019; Akinola & Mendes, 2008). Conceptually speaking, these data introduce questions about the correspondence between the unconscious body and the conscious mind.

With many choices of physiological measures, it can be hard to narrow down a clear hypothesis or research question that explicitly ties the data to other measures and qualitative data. Therefore, it's important to craft a clear rationale (see Chapter 2, Design Essential 2). It's likely that you will need to merge theories to anchor the design, for example theories about physiological processes with theories about psychological processes. If your design includes a quasi-experimental study, then you may also need to consider a third layer—how the physiological processes affecting the psychological processes relate to interpersonal, environmental, or organizational characteristics. For this reason, an experimental component that includes physiological data might be better placed after the other components in a mixed methods study to show the successive building of theory.

Of the various types of experimental mixed methods designs, the physiological design is probably the newest. As an example, Davelaar et al. (2018) included physiological data in a mixed methods study on the topic of neurofeedback. Interviews were conducted with participants after an intervention, and the researchers analyzed differences in subjective experience so it was possible to match interview themes to actions, percepts, and executive functions.

Facilities, equipment, and personnel needed for collecting and analyzing physiological data (electrodermal skin conductance; electroencephalography; eye and facial scanning; neurofeedback data including functional magnetic resonance imaging, functional near-infrared spectroscopy, and magneto-encephalography) can be considerable, especially when layering on top of the typical costs and laboratory space necessary to conduct a traditional experiment. Using electrodes or other devices and equipment can complicate an experimental task. Therefore, it is important to pilot test the task and to make sure the equipment is working properly and that the participants are comfortable with it. The exact timing of each task needs to be monitored, and instructions must be provided to participants.

A flow chart of the specific tasks as well as diagram of brain activity can be helpful when reporting results (see Vásquez-Rosati et al., 2019). The physiological data can tell researchers about the association between an area of the brain or a bodily activity and a specific cognitive function during a task. Researchers try to understand how the physiological data are tied to a function or perception, which then might shape how people set goals, perform a task in a certain way, or develop a social dynamic, for example. In the qualitative interview component, participants can be asked to reflect on these goals, tasks, or dynamics.

STEPS

Figure 5.1 shows the design steps for experimental mixed methods research. Typically, designing the experiment is the primary step because the intervention is the central component of the project. However, as noted in the figure, some experimental mixed methods projects begin with an exploratory interview phase for assisting in the design of the intervention, in which case Step 1 can be swapped with Step 2.

Step 1: Designing the Experiment

Designing the experiment or intervention using rigorous standards of integrity and quality control takes careful planning. Experimental mixed methods designs can be complex and can include a lot of details to plan, more than

FIGURE 5.1. Design Steps for Experimental Mixed Methods Research

Step 1	Step 2	Step 3
Designing the experiment or intervention	**Using the qualitative method before, during, or after the intervention**	**Merging intervention or experiment and interview results**

Data collection: Planning the type and order of tasks for the intervention and control groups	*Design and data collection*: Collect interview data	*Calculate the intervention results*: ANOVA MANCOVA Multiple regression
Piloting any necessary equipment	*Data analysis*: Thematizing narrative experiences from interview data	

Example merge: Explanations of effects (themes) concerning the levels of ratings (descriptive statistics) and significant predictors of experience (multiple regression) compared across groups (ANOVA)

Note. Step 2 would occur first if the interviews are to be used to design the intervention. ANOVA = analysis of variance; MANCOVA = multivariate analysis of covariance.

sequential and convergent mixed methods designs might. If you plan to publish in a mixed methods or general social science journal, as opposed to a psychological journal, readers might be new to experimental research but familiar with mixed methods research. That's why it's important to include all the details and to make sure you clearly describe the experimental procedures so that they make sense, flow well, and don't confuse the reader.

Deciding the Number, Type, and Duration of Conditions

First, it's important to decide how many arms of an intervention or conditions in an experimental or quasi-experimental mixed methods design are necessary. The number depends on the research topic, theories in a research area, and the comparisons you'd like to draw across treatment and control groups. For example, when planning their experimental mixed methods research project, Parke et al. (2021) used the literature to determine the number and type of conditions for promoting organizational change behavior (OCB)—three conditions: supervisor, peers and supervisors, and peers. On the other extreme, Bennett et al. (2020) planned for nine conditions to thoroughly test how employees would react to different types of microbreaks at work. They went to great lengths to use nine conditions to adequately address the lack of clarity in past studies of the effects of microbreak durations.

The duration of an intervention is also important in field studies and collaborations with a liaison in a company, school, clinic, or other provider or organization. How long an intervention should be depends on the type of change you expect to elicit and your design (i.e., if you are doing a counter-balanced design or a time-series design). To estimate how long a planned intervention should be, look at how other researchers conducted their studies and consider the organization's goals and the cognitive load or effort that people can give when participating in the experiment without compromising other aspects of their learning (such as when working with students) or work (such as when working with adults), including duties and other obligations. For example, Parke et al. (2021) used a longitudinal design because they wanted to give participants enough time to "to promote, recognize, and correct performance of OCB" (p. 1715).

Calculating Sample Size and Power

Depending on how many conditions are planned, sample size and power are important to calculate. Considerations include the type of experiment, any industry standards (say, in medical research), and concerns about retention of participants. Dropout rate varies based on type of experiment, and activities affect people differently. For example, Knaust et al. (2022) reported a pooled average dropout rate of 21.9% for virtual reality exposure therapy.

Design Questions: To plan the experiment, ask yourself the following questions:

- Is a laboratory experiment or a quasi-experimental design in the field (e.g., workplace, classroom, school) best suited for the research topic and research questions or hypotheses?

- What type of conditions suit the study, how many should be used, how long should they be?

- What independent, dependent, and/or covariate variables are appropriate?

- What measures are the most appropriate for the study in the particular field?

- For experiments, is it possible to randomly sample participants? How will I randomly assign them to conditions (i.e., treatments and the control group)?

- For quasi-experiments, would it be appropriate to use a counterbalanced or time-series design? Is there a control group that can be used?

- What facilities, equipment, and personnel are needed to set up and administer the intervention(s)?

Step 2: Using Qualitative Interview Methods Before, During, or After an Intervention

As you deliberate about the choices for setting up, planning, and conducting an experiment or quasi-experiment, think about the qualitative interview methods that would best strengthen its design. Of the types of qualitative methods, interviews are most frequently paired with interventions, and semistructured and structured interviews are the most common types of interview. Unstructured or dyadic interviews are not typically used because it is hard to align the data with individual participant data from the intervention.

Sometimes, multiple interviews are completed over time to assess the short-term and long(er) term effects of an intervention. As with other types of interview research, it is important to be clear with participants about confidentiality and anonymity, including the use of pseudonyms. Exclude identifying information such as names, addresses, and employers as well as names and information about other people that may be disclosed during the interview. For more information on common interview practices, including how to record interviews and code them, you may want to refer to qualitative research methods books (see Katz-Buonincontro, 2022, or other books for a quick guide).

Sampling From an Intervention

In experimental mixed methods studies, the issue of how to sample potential interview participants from an intervention sample is often overlooked. Some researchers randomly sample participants from the intervention sample, whereas other researchers ask for volunteers. The key question is whether the study could benefit from representation across both the control and intervention groups or the entire quasi-experimental group. If so, then you can purposefully collect interview data from all groups who participated in the intervention. In addition, the placement of the interviews may help you decide whom to sample.

When to Conduct Interviews

In experimental mixed methods designs, interviews can be conducted before, during, or after an intervention. Table 5.3 provides a comparison of these interview types.

Interviews before an experiment.   When placed before the experiment, interviews with participants help investigators to tailor interventions specific to that group of participants. This early placement of interviews allows investigators to get a baseline sense of participants' attitudes, beliefs, and lived experiences, especially regarding specific challenges such as workplace stress or healthcare barriers. The interview results can then shape the type of interventions that can be developed and used—interview research provides authenticity and legitimacy for interventions (Bennett et al., 2020) and lays the groundwork for crafting hypotheses and research questions. For example, in their experimental mixed methods project, Rogers et al. (2019) developed a culturally specific approach that started with qualitative focus groups and ended with interviews to develop a new intervention for colorectal cancer (CRC) screening for African American men. The research team used an innovative strategy to select the research sites, barbershops located in Salt Lake City, Utah, and Minneapolis–St. Paul, Minnesota. The rationale for using barbershops was to recruit African American men as participants by enhancing their comfort with being around others of a similar age who had not yet been screened for CRC. In another project, Parke et al. (2021) conducted 60 interviews with managers at a large corporation to see what organizational change behaviors they valued. Once the behaviors were identified, the researchers mapped the behaviors to theory. Then, the intervention was designed.

Interviews during an experiment.   Interviews with participants during an intervention can provide critical feedback on the experiences related to the intervention. Sometimes the word "interview" is used in experimental research to simply check in with the study participants, but interviews are really meant to tease out the thoughts, beliefs, and perspectives related to the participant experience going through a specific treatment, beyond a simple check-in. Treatment effects can be further delineated and contrasted with the inclusion of interview data.

Interviews after an experiment.   In experimental mixed methods designs, interviews are most commonly conducted after a trial, intervention, or treatment to help explain the quantitative results. Investigators wait until after the intervention is complete to interview participants because they do not

TABLE 5.3. Using Interviews Before, During, or After Interventions

			Placement of interviews	
			(C) After intervention	
	(A) Before intervention	**(B) During intervention**	**Immediately after**	**Delayed (months after)**
Purpose	To design the intervention using interview outcomes	To ascertain any side-effects or other experiences	To debrief participants To confirm accuracy of participant responses To explain experiences To confirm or disconfirm intervention effects	To understand longer term intervention effects
Duration	15–30 minutes	15–30 minutes	15–30 minutes	30 minutes or more
Affordances	Legitimizing and authenticating the development of the intervention Crafting the hypotheses and research questions	Describing experiences as they occur	Illuminating the direct impact of intervention	Understanding delayed effects and outcomes
Challenges	Not using the sample intended to receive the intervention(s)	Planning when to interview so as to not interrupt the treatment	Unforeseen delays can make it hard to get firsthand impressions Inadequate representation of participants from each condition	Continued access to participants after the interventions

want to contaminate ongoing interventions. For example, Liu et al. (2020) interviewed older adults and college students to compare their experiences using virtual reality after an experiment that tested their perceived telepresence, video preference, and viewing experience. Li and Xu (2019) likewise interviewed study participants after an intervention testing the efficacy of emotional intelligence activities. Interview protocols can be crafted to learn about the participants' experience in the control group versus that of participants in the intervention group(s), and different sets of questions can be posed, depending on the type of intervention. Postintervention interviews are typically relatively short, about 15 to 30 minutes in duration.

When interviews are performed immediately after the intervention to give direct feedback to investigators, they are sometimes called exit interviews. Also known as debriefing interviews, exit interviews offer participants a chance to discuss the pros and cons of their intervention experience (Rogers et al., 2019), their likes and dislikes, and areas for improvement (Kim & Lim, 2013). Exit interviews can elicit the study participants' reactions to various experimental procedures, such as the presence of a voice guiding participants through a coloring experiment (Mantzios & Giannou, 2018). In contrast, delayed postintervention interviews are conducted several months after the intervention to follow up with participants (Rogers et al., 2019).

Design Questions: Consider how you will integrate qualitative data into your project by asking yourself the following questions:

- Should I place the qualitative methods before, during, or after the intervention?
- Would either exit/debriefing or delayed interviews serve the study better?
- How will I sample interview participants from the intervention sample?
- Are interviews or focus groups better suited for the project?
- Will I design separate interview protocols for the control and intervention groups?

Step 3: Merging the Quantitative and the Qualitative Results

Merging the quantitative and the qualitative results begins with calculating the outcome(s) of the intervention. Next, the narrative-based experiences generated from the qualitative data are grouped into themes. Finally, the results are compared to identify ways they reinforce each other or, conversely, diverge.

Calculating Intervention Results

Computing the results of the quantitative phase of the study requires selecting and running the appropriate statistical tests for your experiment, followed by reporting the findings. To determine the appropriateness of various inferential statistical analyses, consider which type of analysis matches your research questions and hypotheses. For example, comparing means across two or more groups may require analysis of variance (ANOVA), comparing two or more dependent variables across groups may use multivariate analysis of variance (MANOVA), and controlling for extraneous variables and adjusting posttest scores for initial differences on a variable may require multivariate analysis of covariance (MANCOVA), depending on issues such as random assignment to treatment groups (cf. Gay et al., 2009). Multiple regression may be used to test whether one variable predicts another. For in-depth steps to perform statistical analyses, consult a statistics book such as Green and Salkind (2017), Salkind (2017), or Tanner (2012).

Design Questions: To begin Step 1, think about the 10 essential design features of mixed methods research introduced in Chapter 1 and consider the weighting of the quantitative and qualitative data:

- How will I calculate the intervention effects?
- Which statistical test helps address my hypotheses and/or quantitative research question?
- How do the experiment or quasi-experiment results relate to the interview results?

Thematizing Narrative-Based Experiences

Analysis of intervention data typically, though not always, results in themes elucidating (narrative-based) experiences either before, during, or after the intervention. If interview data are collected and analyzed to assist in designing the intervention, then the interview data analysis would occur as the first or second step rather than as the last step. Themes can be organized around people's experiences, thoughts, feelings, or processes going through the intervention. Other interview analyses highlight characterizing changes over time.

Evidence that intervention activities affect participants can be collected via self-report open-ended questionnaires and then analyzed from interviews with extracted themes and supporting quotes. Some researchers choose to thematize the interviews, which provide validity and targeted evidence better than stand-alone quotes do. Other researchers provide quotes that couple with the quantitative results, which suffices for some journal reporting standards. For example, Li and Xu (2019) reported quotes on the positive change in emotional behavior by using quotes that linked to this theme:

> I am definitely sure that I will make it a habit to reflect on my emotional skills and emotional experiences, not only in English learning but also in my daily life. Thanks to the training, I find myself stronger and happier. (Xiowang [pseudonym]; p. 12)

The positive emotions articulated in this quoted passage correspond to analysis of covariance results indicating an increase in self-rated emotional intelligence after a six-week training.

Design Questions: As you analyze the qualitative interview data, think about how it relates back to the intervention or experiment as the predominant data source:

- How do the interview results expressed as themes and quotes relate to the experiment results?

- For treatments and interventions, do the interviews confirm either the efficacy or the inefficacy of the treatment?

- With respect to different types of conditions, how do the interviews explain or expand on the differences in participant scores?

SUMMARY

Chapter 5 introduced the basic concepts of mixed methods designs that include either an experimental or a quasi-experimental design component. Four main types of this design—basic, case study, arts-based, and physiological—are uniquely applied; the chapter includes suggestions and ways to plan for them. As these designs have evolved over time, there will surely be more innovations in this area. The steps for designing mixed methods experimental research were provided in this chapter, placing the experiment at the heart of the design: This type of mixed methods design will always prioritize the quantitative data collection and analysis, in contrast to sequential and convergent mixed methods designs. Qualitative interview data are usually collected after the experiment, though some projects include interviews before an experiment—to design an intervention, for example—or during an experiment.

As experimental mixed methods designs follow rigorous steps that meet the validity standards of general experimental work, the next chapter addresses the question of how a mixed methods project, taken as a whole, would address validity from a mixed methods perspective in which both quantitative and qualitative validity are considered together. Though I have lightly discussed the demonstration of quantitative and qualitative data through what mixed methods researchers call integration, I discuss this and other matters, such as the construction of joint displays, more in depth in Chapter 6.

6

VALIDITY, INTEGRATION, AND JOINT DISPLAYS

So far, this book has covered the three major mixed methods designs (sequential, convergent, and experimental). With these fundamentals under your belt, it's time to look more deeply at ways to ensure methodological integrity and to learn about validity, integration, and joint displays. Strategizing ways to address these key elements will take your mixed methods project from good to publishable (articles) or winning (grants).

You're probably familiar with the terms "validity" and "reliability" as used in social science research methods. Both quantitative and qualitative researchers look for ways to sufficiently establish validity. Other terms for validity are "verification," "accuracy," "authenticity," and "trustworthiness." Reliability is also referred to as "dependability" and "consistency." So, you might be wondering, are there any special features of validity and reliability to examine in the context of mixed methods research design? Of these two concepts, mixed methods scholars focus more on ways to conceptualize validity that are unique to mixed methods research than they focus on reliability. To that end, this chapter provides a foundational understanding of seven mixed methods validity strategies. I'll also provide a quick refresher on reliability techniques.

https://doi.org/10.1037/0000404-007
How to Mix Methods: A Guide to Sequential, Convergent, and Experimental Research Designs, by J. Katz-Buonincontro

Related to validity, the concept of integration is a hot mixed methods topic. Integration refers to the options for deftly merging quantitative and qualitative data. Some mixed methods books refer to integration lightly or do not clarify the junctures at which integration can occur because the term has changed so much over the past few years. This chapter describes four types of integration.

In addition to writing about integration in a narrative format, researchers design visual or graphic displays, which sparks an interest in playing with data creatively (discussed in Chapter 1) while meeting the standards of data representation (American Psychological Association, 2020). So, to round out your skills in validity and integration, Chapter 6 includes ways to use simple and complex joint displays that use numerical and text-based data to demonstrate integration. You'll get lots of inspiration for displaying your results in a figure or table format.

This chapter includes seven mixed methods validity strategies that can help make your project clear and easy to defend, describe, and publish. In addition, the chapter presents information about the integration of qualitative and quantitative data at different points in the mixed methods research cycle: sampling integration, data collection integration, analysis integration, and results integration. Three types of joint displays provide some creative and interesting choices for displaying your data.

METHODOLOGICAL INTEGRITY

With the increase in mixed methods research, there's been an uptick in articles suggesting strategies to address methodological integrity and ways to establish validity. Validity is concerned with the careful conceptualization, collection, and analysis of data using standardized principles of research practice to ensure quality, accuracy, and transparency in the research cycle and research outcomes. It's commonplace in quantitative research to address threats to internal, external, construct, and statistical conclusion validity (Cook & Campbell, 1979). In qualitative research, validity centers on trustworthiness and authenticity (Lincoln & Guba, 1985). Scholars may prefer not to use the word "validity" when discussing qualitative research because the chief concern about methodological integrity lies in the accuracy of the representation of lived experiences, voices, and stories.

In keeping with this history of documenting validity in the social, health, and behavioral sciences, mixed methods researchers maintain the importance of outlining validity strategies. What makes validity in mixed methods research different than forms of validity in other social science research? Good question! Essentially, mixed methods validity builds on key definitions of validity to describe how rigor is supported when a researcher uses both quantitative and qualitative methods. A distinguishing concern of mixed methods researchers is the ability to establish the reader's faith and trust that the results are defensible and are seen as legitimate (Collins et al., 2012). Initially, the terms "triangulation," "complementarity," "development," "expansion," and "initiation" were used to describe validity strategies (Greene et al., 1989). Over time, additional validity terms evolved, as discussed in the next section.

MIXED METHODS VALIDITY STRATEGIES

Seven conceptions of mixed methods validity are summarized in Table 6.1. Although many validity strategies have similar surface-level features, when choosing among these seven strategies, select the strategy that best fits your project. Strategies can shift as your project develops. For example, you may need to accommodate the type of data you've collected, the needs of a community, the demands of a dissertation committee, or the requirements for a grant.

When contemplating a validity strategy, ask yourself the following question:

- Which validity strategy or strategies best addresses my positionality, data collection approach, and/or data analysis strategies?

Strategy 1: Triangulation

Triangulation has come to be a catch-all word, used to mean connecting and looking for similarities across both qualitative and quantitative results. Originally in the context of the multitrait–multimethod design, Webb et al. (1966) stated,

> once a proposition has been confirmed by two or more independent measurement processes, the uncertainty of its interpretation is greatly reduced. The most persuasive evidence comes through a triangulation of measurement processes. (p. 3)

TABLE 6.1. Seven Mixed Methods Validity Strategies

Strategy	Definition	Origins of strategy	Examples
Triangulation	Comparison of results within and across qualitative and quantitative results	Looking for patterns across multiple data sources, theories and researcher perspectives (Jick, 1979)	Sequencing data across time or repeating interviews and surveys in waves (Flick, 2018)
Complementarity	Elaboration or enhancement of the results from one method (Phase 1) to inform data collection (Phase 2)	Recognizing that measurement constrains phenomena and individual experience informs measurement (Carroll & Rothe, 2010) Developing contextual evidence to support the principle of thick description (Geertz, 1973)	Weaving quantitative and qualitative results together in themes (Fetters et al., 2013)
Development	Results inform the development of another method	Developing codes and refining concepts (Merriam, 2009)	Validating a quantitative instrument with crossover analysis Using factors from exploratory factor analysis for thematic analysis of interview data (Onwuegbuzie et al., 2010)
Expansion	Enlarging the inquiry by adding new data	Obtaining a longitudinal perspective and immersing oneself in the data to extend and prolong the inquiry (Merriam, 2009)	Completing quantitative analysis and using the results to develop an interview protocol for a second phase of data collection and analysis

Term			
Initiation	Identifying paradoxes that lead to a new research question	Examining data for discrepant or contradictory evidence (Merriam, 2009)	Using paradoxes that emerge from qualitative data to generate hypotheses (Polachek & Wallace, 2018)
Liberation (also called transformation or emancipation)	Bringing to light silenced or oppressed voices through research	Focusing on lives and experience of those who have been oppressed (Mertens, 2003) Using a feminist lens to promote social justice through describing power, gender, and control (Hesse-Biber, 2010)	Exposing hidden silences through oral histories and discrepancies with quantitative data (Nightingale, 2006)
Cultural Relevance	Also called cultural coconstruction, flexibly adapting to cultural context	Cultural responsiveness, Indigenous knowledge, co-creation of research projects that are socially valid from a community's perspective	Mixed methods psychological interventions that balance scientific knowledge (standardization) with Indigenous knowledge (contextualization) (Nastasi & Hitchcock, 2016)

Note. The first five terms are derived from Greene et al. (1989). Liberation strategies were developed from feminist and social justice frameworks such as Hesse-Biber (2010).

As noted in Chapter 1, triangulation as a popular turn of phrase used in social research and especially in the earlier years of mixed methods research is based on Jick's (1979) term for establishing multiple lines of sight, adapted from the Air Force field. Denzin (1978) extended the term to sociological methods and the wider field of qualitative research.

Why is this strategy based on the shape of a triangle, implying three separate data sources or independent measures? The triangles outlining similar results in a correlation matrix came to stand as symbols for finding patterns of similarities across multiple independent measures (Bazeley & Kemp, 2012). Denzin (1978), a qualitative researcher, further elaborated on the concept to include triangulation at the theoretical level. Jick (1979) noted that triangulation has positive psychological benefits for the researcher: They can feel more confident in the results and provide more creative avenues.

There has never been a one-size-fits-all approach to triangulation. Rather, triangulation can be achieved in many ways. Though triangulation depends on the aims and methods of the research project, it cannot be assumed in any mixed methods study. The onus is on the researcher to tell the story of how triangulation is or is not achieved or is not possible. Explaining triangulation is important for establishing rigor, especially when journal guidelines are unclear. Such explanations can be helpful in the context of justifying mixed methods research that has high costs in terms of personnel (e.g., multiple observers) or requires prolonged time in the field (Kadushin et al., 2008).

Greene and McClintock (1985) described how between-method triangulation strengthens the methodology of concurrent mixed methods evaluations in which questionnaires (quantitative research) provide structure to the evaluation and interviews (qualitative research) provide description and integrity. Flick (2018) noted that mixed methods researchers can sequence or use data across time, repeating interviews and surveys in phases or waves. Triangulation can be viewed as comparing causal claims about mechanical causality (changes in behavior, measured quantitatively) with agentic causality (intention behind the behavior, researched qualitatively; cf. Howe, 2012). So, to conclude, triangulation can be referenced in any type of mixed methods design. Tips to achieve triangulation include

- Conducting interviews to describe people's reasons (qualitative data) for the choices they made when providing ratings (quantitative data).

- Repeating interviews to look at verifying themes over time, across experiences, and across participants, cases, or sites.

- Using time-series designs to collect quantitative data about experience in a longitudinal manner to see how data might change over time.

Strategy 2: Complementarity

Complementarity is a frequently used mixed methods term, referring to elaborating on one set of results (e.g., qualitative) with another set of results (e.g., quantitative). This principle is quite popular in mixed methods research (Bazeley & Kemp, 2012). The quantitative and qualitative data can be presented as themes to advance greater conceptual coherence and can be presented together in the Results section of a paper (Fetters et al., 2013). This strategy for ensuring validity has origins in how measurement informs experience (Carroll & Rothe, 2010) and how contextual details help verify claims, as is the case with the principle of thick description (see Geertz, 1973). "Thick description" is a term derived from ethnographic research that has since been used in the social sciences to refer to a method for providing sufficient detail about the possible intentions underlying human behavior as a basis of validity. Thick description originally referred to many layers of interpretation in field research as conveyed through observations:

> a multiplicity of complex conceptual structures, many of them superimposed upon or knotted into one another, which are at once strange, irregular, and inexplicit, and which he must contrive somehow first to grasp and then to render. (Geertz, 1973, p. 10)

Complementarity is a good mixed methods validity strategy if you are using a convergent mixed methods design that uses multiple sources of data to obtain a unified picture of an understudied topic. The researcher would be investigating how, for example, social media, emails, policies, and blogs might complement the commonly used survey, assessment, and interview data (Bazeley & Kemp, 2012). For example, Simões et al. (2005) collected three types of data together in the first phase of their convergent mixed methods study: published documents, in-depth interviews, and materials from tourism and hotel industry events to understand issues including corporate brand development and service identity.

Bazeley and Kemp (2012, p. 58) suggest complementarity for

- Combining data for completion
- Combining data for enhancement
- Combining data to detail a more significant whole

Strategy 3: Development

Development differs from complementarity. An example of development as a validity strategy is crossover analysis, the process for validating a quantitative instrument that uses a thematic analysis of interview data based on factors from an exploratory factor analysis (Onwuegbuzie et al., 2010). Development reflects the social scientific tradition of refining and characterizing codes (Merriam, 2009). Development is a good mixed methods validity strategy for a researcher who is using an exploratory sequential mixed methods design in which qualitative interview data (Phase 1) are used to develop an instrument (Phase 2). For example, Agans et al. (2006) developed a culturally sensitive approach to investigating Mexican immigrant women's experiences with menstruation. First, the researchers noticed a lack of Spanish-language instruments and a lack of cultural sensitivity among researchers working on this topic with women. Thus, they used focus groups to discuss women's concerns and better understand the nuances of cultural taboos and experiences with menstruation, such as medical misdiagnoses due to racism. Then, they drafted a new questionnaire based on the themes emerging from the focus groups.

Development can be used as a validity strategy when

- Developing a new instrument
- Developing an intervention

Strategy 4: Expansion

Expansion is the extension of one phase with another phase in a mixed methods study. For example, an explanatory sequential mixed methods study might first include a survey of participants (Phase 1); the researchers might then analyze the survey data and develop an interview protocol for additional data collection and analysis (Phase 2). This strategy is rooted in immersion and prolonged fieldwork (Merriam, 2009). Therefore, you might not know what the second phase of the project is until you are immersed in fieldwork. Expansion can show the tight coherence or linkage across phases of research, for example when developing a hypothesis based on qualitative observations (Phase 1) and then testing that hypothesis with quantitative observations (Phase 2).

Kadushin et al. (2008) attempted to expand poorly correlated ratings (participant ratings and observer ratings of tour bus drivers) with field observations. They first observed people on a tour and noticed that good guides helped people focus and share their experiences. Next, they formed a focal experience hypothesis; observers then ranked tour bus guides on their performance in terms of achieving cohesion and community. In this way, expansion helped to clarify and then expand on findings from the first set of data.

Expansion can be a suitable mixed methods validity strategy for an explanatory sequential mixed methods design. In particular, expansion can be used as a validity strategy when

- Extending survey data with interview data
- Adding a phase of data collection based on the unexpected results from the first phase of data

Strategy 5: Initiation

Initiation occurs when the data suggest a paradox. Initiation is perhaps the least likely used type of mixed methods validity because it involves examining data for discrepant or contradictory evidence (Merriam, 2009). It can be a relevant validity strategy when there is an impasse in understanding the results (Bazeley & Kemp, 2012), causing the researchers to go back to the drawing board to create new variables or survey new informants in a larger study. The initiation validity strategy can be well suited to exploratory sequential mixed methods designs focusing on social justice or designs that are exploratory in nature.

In an example of the use of initiation, Polachek and Wallace (2018) conducted interviews with veterinarians and animal health technicians to address the issue of how provider–client–patient interactions relate to compassion satisfaction and compassion fatigue. They were careful to interleave hypotheses after identifying qualitative themes, as shown:

- Qualitative Interview Theme 1: Satisfying interactions (provider–client–patients)
  - Hypothesis 1 derived from Theme 1: Making a difference to animals will be positively associated with compassion satisfaction.
  - Hypothesis 2 derived from Theme 1: Building relationships with animals and human clients will be positively associated with compassion satisfaction.
- Qualitative Interview Theme 2: Stressful interactions (provider–client–patients)
  - Hypothesis 3 derived from Theme 2: Barriers to animal care will be positively associated with compassion fatigue.
  - Hypothesis 4 derived from Theme 2: Witnessing suffering and death will be positively associated with compassion fatigue. (Polachek & Wallace, 2018, pp. 232–234)

These hypotheses then shaped the quantitative stage of their mixed methods research study, including the selection of a compassion fatigue scale and a larger, secondary sample of veterinarians and animal care technicians.

Bazeley and Kemp (2012) suggested generation and initiation for

- Initiating a new line of inquiry
- Paradoxical data that call for starting a new phase

Strategy 6: Liberation, Transformation, or Emancipation

As discussed in Chapter 1, many mixed methods researchers aim to foster social, educational, or health progress. Liberation—also called transformation or emancipation—validity strategies amplify silenced, oppressed, or marginalized voices (Hesse-Biber, 2012; Mertens, 2003). The qualitative genre of narrative research using oral histories can be used to explore discrepancies within quantitative data (Nightingale, 2003, as cited in Hesse-Biber, 2012). The dissonance between the quantitative data and the qualitative data can highlight and potentially uncover social truths that might otherwise be dismissed or ignored as valid.

For example, Vikström (2003) found that women engaged in work outside the home during a time when they were expected to be domestic. The data were not recorded in official registers, implying that the women's work was not seen as officially valid and thus legitimate in society. But in actuality, this study suggested that women's work contributed to their subsistence and perhaps even other factors critical to family and personal well-being and economic prosperity. As seen in this example, liberation can be a suitable mixed methods validity strategy for mixed methods designs with a social justice and/or a feminist focus.

Liberation, transformation, or emancipation can be used as a validity strategy when the researcher is

- Drawing attention to people who have experienced oppression, violence, minoritization, or gaslighting relative to the rest of society

- Highlighting qualitative data that might have been obfuscated by the quantitative data

Strategy 7: Cultural Relevance

Adhering to the cultural and social rigor of a project and its context constitutes a form of validity. Mixed methods projects with cultural relevance deliberately include people's Indigenous knowledge and the cocreation of research projects that are socially valid from a community's perspective. Nastasi and Hitchcock (2016) discussed mixed methods psychological interventions that balance scientific knowledge (standardization) with Indigenous knowledge (contextualization). Some mixed methods researchers take positionality (reflecting on and writing about one's relationship with partners and research participants, as outlined in Chapter 1) a step further to deliberately codevelop interventions with community members. Cultural coconstruction is the method by which researchers work with community members as partners developing interventions that acknowledge real-life experiences in communities (Nastasi & Hitchcock, 2016).

Coconstruction is an example of the first mixed methods design principle, valuing multiple truths (see Chapter 1). For example, a mixed methods research team might realize they need to adjust, adapt, or pilot an instrument that has been standardized and normed in White communities for use in a specific cultural context. As a result, the researchers might engage community members in interviews (qualitative) and then adapt an instrument based on those interviews to pilot with another sample of community participants (quantitative). This approach would be an exploratory sequential design. Cultural coconstruction highlights how rigor arises out of working with community members in the research design, not just in the data collection process.

Cultural relevance can be used as a validity strategy when

- Deliberately focusing on intersectional and cultural identities of both the participants and the researchers
- Emphasizing collaboration with community research partners

MEMBER CHECKING OR RESPONDENT VALIDATION

Validity is concerned with truthfulness and accuracy of research. Verifying data reports with community members who are collaborators and with study participants is also core to mixed methods research. Member checking is a term used predominantly in qualitative research to address the process of sharing transcriptions, data analysis, and/or results with participants to ensure fairness and ethics in the representation of voices and narratives to the wider public.

An important trend in mixed methods research is extending this concept of member checking or respondent validation to use at the local level or in an organization (Brown et al., 2015; Torrance, 2012). If either social justice or advancing society to make progress are the main aims of a mixed methods project, then an important part of the validation process is to work with people to see how they can use the research resulting from the study. Because the field of mixed methods has strong roots in the field of program evaluation, working with participants to improve the quality of programs and their effectiveness is important (see Davidov et al., 2020).

RELIABILITY

Reliability is an important concept in social science research. However, it's not commonly discussed in mixed methods scholarship as a special form of reliability separate from how it is treated in qualitative and quantitative methods. Reliability refers to the precision, clarity, and fidelity of how data are conceptualized, collected, and analyzed. Mixed methods researchers use both quantitative and qualitative forms of reliability.

In quantitative research, three main types of reliability exist. Computation of interrater reliability involves at least two independent observers rating the same product, and they are blind to each other's scores. A correlation coefficient such as Cronbach's alpha is used to examine the degree of similarity across multiple raters' scores. Test–retest reliability examines the stability of participant scores on a test or survey at independent points in time. Internal consistency reliability looks at the degree to which different items on a specific scale interrelate.

Qualitative reliability strategies include striving for consistency, dependability, and transparency of data. Coding transcriptions comprehensively is another form of reliability. Some qualitative researchers use interrater reliability when teams code transcriptions or opt to emphasize difference in interpretation across team members who code the same transcription, depending on the project and researchers' positionality. For example, some researchers might choose to code with several research team members and research partners and do not stress a single interpretation of the data.

Finally, the concept of transferability is considered by many qualitative researchers as important for tracking lessons from contexts to apply or adapt to new contexts, whereas quantitative researchers value generalizability. Historically, both quantitative and qualitative social scientists have been concerned with not overgeneralizing results (Merriam, 2009) so that they are not sensitized to situations (Glaser & Strauss, 1967). Therefore, "transferability" is a term that refers to the congruence, fittingness, or similarity between findings in one context and another (Lincoln & Guba, 1985, as cited in Patton, 2002).

INTEGRATION

Once you choose and describe a validity strategy or strategies that best fit your mixed methods project and explain reliability, you're ready to embark on data analysis and the integration of the results. What does integration mean, and why do mixed methods researchers need to address it in their projects? Integration is what makes mixed methods research projects unique from single-method projects. Tunarosa and Glynn (2017) defined integration as the process of "crafting a logical, credible explanation by construing novel associations across quantitative and qualitative elements" (p. 239).

Integration is a term that hasn't been used until recently in the field of mixed methods. The purpose of integration is to emphasize the mixing of two or more strands of data, instead of noting or describing them separately. In Chapter 1, Table 1.1, multimethod research stressed multideterminism as a scientific philosophy, but multimethod research does not go so far as to purposefully sequence, mix, and interpret data. In early years, mixed methods research was criticized for looking a bit like multimethod research. Sometimes the terms mixed methods and multimethod research were used interchangeably in language. Older mixed methods projects did not have a Comparison section. Now, the current standard of practice is to provide a section comparing the quantitative and qualitative results. Therefore, it is important to explain the type of data analysis used for both qualitative and quantitative data sets (see American Psychological Association, 2020, for the mixed methods article reporting standards).

Because it's uncommon for researchers to have formal training in mixed methods, they sometimes report qualitative and quantitative results without examining them in relation to one another (Bryman, 2007). Occasionally, researchers compare the methods in the Discussion section (see Kim & Lim, 2013), and some articles do not refer to integration at all (see Bartholomew & Lockard, 2018). To address the variation in reporting practices, scholars have laid out frameworks for "points of integration" (Schoonenboom & Johnson, 2017), degrees of integration (Lynam et al., 2020), and fully integrated mixed methods research (Creamer, 2018). In summary, your work will be perceived as rigorous when several if not all forms of integration are used in your research process and explained in your research writing.

As integration is the intentional comparison of the quantitative and qualitative data sets after individual analyses are completed, I don't review every type of qualitative and quantitative data analysis procedure in this chapter. Rather, I describe four junctures to consider integration: sampling, data collection, data analysis, and presenting results. To complement this chapter, you may want to refer to textbooks for in-depth information on specific techniques (for an overview of quantitative data analysis techniques, see Salkind, 2017; for an overview of qualitative data analysis techniques, see Katz-Buonincontro, 2022).

Integration Type 1: Sampling Integration

Sampling integration is a sampling process in which the researcher selects the participants for Phase 2 that is a subset of the sample for Phase 1. Sampling integration can occur when collecting data with large samples used in the initial phase of a mixed methods study. Ideally, researchers should review the quantitative and qualitative sampling strategies to make sure they are clear in your mind before progressing to the stage of sampling integration. Based on the types of responses, a relatively smaller number of participants can be sampled for other data such as interviews or focus groups. For example, a study of sex attitudes and practices provided clusters of participants, which were then further sampled (Nickel et al., 1995). Bartholomew and Lockard (2018) noted that many psychotherapy mixed methods articles use the same sample for the qualitative component or use a secondary set of participants from the larger sample based on cut-off scores.

Stratified sampling of participants can also provide specific and clear criteria based on type or level of participant experience. For example, Fitzpatrick (2016) selected a subset of music teachers from a survey sample of music teachers, based on their level of experience and the quality of the music program (described as struggling or thriving). Although the sampling criteria may at first appear subjective, Fitzpatrick examined the number of music performances and perceived excellence by the community to categorize a program as thriving or struggling. As such, the criteria and choice for selecting the qualitative sample from the quantitative sample was based on defensible logic.

Design question: To achieve sampling integration, ask yourself,

- What is a sound rationale for selecting participants from the original, larger sample used in Phase 1 of my project?

Integration Type 2: Data Collection Integration

Data collection integration refers to the process of allowing participants to opt into data collection. This approach can be particularly important when researchers aim to include minoritized communities and want to design culturally sensitive studies. Social processes inherent in integration affect data collection (Lynam et al., 2020), and thus the quality of relationships bear on and affect the quality of data. That is, an instrument may need to be translated into a different language, and researchers may need to work with the right set of professionals who have built strong relationships with the communities that include the research participants for the mixed methods study. In addition, the construct of interest should focus the data collection integration. Plano Clark (2019) recommended charting out the data collection instrument and protocols to see how well they match and correspond to the construct of interest. Table 6.2 expands on Plano Clark's example construct of interest, teacher use of praise.

Design questions: To achieve data collection integration, ask yourself,

- How does the qualitative data and the quantitative data represent the same construct of interest?

- If the planned data collection instruments do not represent the same construct of interest, how might I adjust the instruments or change them?

Integration Type 3: Analysis Integration

Analysis integration is a process in which the analysis of one phase of the mixed methods study affects the type of analysis used in a later phase of the mixed methods study. Analysis integration occurs in waves, wherein one wave serves as the basis for making the next data analysis decision, as

TABLE 6.2. Data Collection Integration Example

Construct	Teacher use of praise	Type of behavior	Type of data	Time
	Description			
Quantitative representation of construct	Tallies of praise statements made by teachers	Objective praise	Observations	Real-time
Qualitative representation of construct	Teacher interview data on use of praise	Subjective praise	Interviews	Retrospective
Data collection integration	Both sets of data represent teacher use of praise	Comparison of objective and subjective praise	Comparison of observation and interview themes	Comparison of real-time and retrospective behavior

opposed to the data analysis occurring separately for each wave of the study. Though scholars debate whether analyses can truly be integrated when there are differing epistemological underpinnings about the nature of truth and reality (see Uprichard & Dawney, 2019), analysis integration can occur when one type of analysis influences another type of analysis. For example, in crossover analysis, researchers can identify a pattern and then see if that pattern holds up in another data set. In addition to patterns, each data set might represent various levels of an organization, such as policymakers (Level 1), implementers of a policy (Level 2), and users or indirect recipients of a policy (Level 3). The multilevel data sets allow for separate streams of data, implying the potential for comparison.

Flick et al. (2012) used analysis integration in their study. They first examined a quantitative data set to identify the frequency of sleeping problems and correlations with other diagnoses and percentages in the prescription data. Then, the researchers looked at the qualitative data for typologies of attitudes or interpretative patterns. In the third step, they tried to see what relationship the data had to each other.

To further demonstrate the principle of analysis integration, let's look at a study that used four waves of data analysis integration. Using the process of photo-elicitation, Peroff et al. (2020) conducted a mixed methods study in which they provided landscape photographs to interview participants and asked them about their attachment to the landscapes in Guatemala (see Figure 6.1). The authors also used ethnographic field observation to understand the construct of interest, attachment to place. Integration at the data analysis level started with assigning codes derived from the interviews to each landscape photograph. Next, the researchers compared the interview codes to the ethnographic field observation notes. Then, the researchers organized the importance rankings of the photographs by the participants in a spreadsheet. Multidimensional scaling was used to measure the distances between objects (in this case, the photographs) on a matrix. SPSS was used to calculate correlations and to provide a correlation matrix. To achieve data analysis integration, the authors then named the themes based on the statistical clustering that resulted from multidimensional scaling. To summarize, the researchers used the following pattern of data analysis: qualitative data analysis (QDA), two rounds of quantitative data analysis (Qn-DA), ending with QDA [QDA: QnDA: QnDA: QDA].

Design question: To achieve data analysis integration, ask yourself,

- Which data analysis pattern or trend in Phase 1 can organize and guide the data analysis in Phase 2 (as well as any other phases)?

FIGURE 6.1. Data Analysis Integration Example

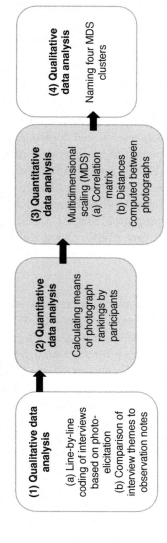

Note. White boxes denote qualitative analyses, and gray boxes denote quantitative analyses.

Integration Type 4: Results Integration

Results integration occurs when two or more separate results are compared and then explicitly linked. Integration can show the connections across results of the qualitative and quantitative data sets (Sligo et al., 2018). As discussed in Chapter 1, results integration flows from a mixed methods research question that explicitly describes the relationship between a quantitative set of results and a qualitative set of results.

Convergence

A powerful strategy used in mixed methods studies is to compare sets of results, derived independently, across multiple samples of participants. For example, Flick et al. (2012) interviewed doctors and nurses separately and found that both groups perceived the treatment of sleeping problems with drugs to be a huge issue. Though they found similarities across these groups, they did not shy away from exposing the differences between doctors and nurses in these attitudes. That is, Flick discovered ambivalence toward using medication to treat sleeping problems. As a next step, Flick followed up these qualitative data with quantitative data to link two separate constructs: attitudes and practices.

Divergence

If divergence is found across two or more data sets, then researchers can build new studies (Schoonenboom & Johnson, 2017). Contradictions across data sets may first feel a little unsettling, so it's good to know that mixed methods research can expose differences and suggest further research to be conducted in the future (Fitzpatrick, 2016). Sometimes surveys elicit reflections on global or general experience rather than specific task- or event-related experience. There are potential reasons why a person might respond to a survey in a way that is different from speaking about their experience in an interview. Divergence can also be explained by errors in design, measurement, other limitations of the study, or theoretical explanation.

Theoretical Explanation

Explanations in differences across quantitative and qualitative data sets can be crafted at the theoretical level in addition to the empirical level. Theoretical explanations can provide a way to integrate the two sets of divergent results by attempting to explain variation. Schoonenboom and Johnson (2017) argued that the theory can touch upon the "sense," or expected result, and the "anti-sense," or unexpected result. Many research articles have a section titled Alternate Explanations, in which the authors wrestle with different aspects of the results in addition to describing past studies that support the hypotheses as well as past studies that refute the hypotheses.

Design questions: To achieve results integration, ask yourself the following questions:

- Are there two or more sets of results that converge and can be linked?
- If not, how do the data sets diverge?
- What theories explain variation, divergence, or convergence across the results?

JOINT DISPLAYS

Joint displays are the most creative aspect of integration and are considered a sign of excellence in mixed methods publications. What's so important about joint displays? The term "joint display" is specific to mixed methods; it refers to graphic displays that purposefully conjoin the quantitative and qualitative (and sometimes visual data, such as photos) together so that the data can be understood. Data presentation in graphic displays is key to audience comprehension (Nicol & Pexman, 2010a).

From tables to figures (e.g., bar graphs, line graphs, charts, maps), graphic displays have conventional features that adhere to common standards. Graphic displays play a key role in the section in which they are mentioned. They should be as simple as possible and include concise labels to facilitate straightforward comprehension in their own right (Nicol & Pexman, 2010a). Visual displays also aim to balance aesthetic qualities with mathematical "truth" to engage people's perception (Putnam et al., 2010). That's where innovations in joint displays come in. Joint displays introduce new ways for visualizing the relationship between quantitative and qualitative data. Not all published mixed methods research has joint displays, but they convey rigor by demonstrating integration.

Option 1: Side-by-Side Tables

A basic and common joint display is a relatively simple side-by-side table (see Guetterman et al., 2021), sometimes called a matrix, that is read from left to right. It has columns for quantitative and qualitative results and an additional column that presents meta-inferences, interpretations of how the data reflect each other, with compatibilities and dissimilarities.

How do we figure out which data to use and how to organize it into a clear joint display? Organizing a side-by-side table depends on the mixed methods research project. The table can eventually be organized by research question, case, person, profile, independent variables, or themes (Tashakkori et al., 2021), but a simple way to start is to list data for quantitative and qualitative data sets in separate columns (Johnson et al., 2019). Consider whether and how to notate aspects such as missing data or miscoded data. Once data are listed in columns, parallels across the two columns can be discerned. Some data comparisons may not be appropriate and/or effective in a visual display, and in those situations you can make editorial decisions as to which data to present in the joint display. An important thing to remember is that data can be left in separate stand-alone charts, tables, and figures— not all data need to fit into a joint display, but the major overlapping findings and results should be included.

Joint displays typically include meta-inferences, a mixed methods interpretation, in a final table column. Meta-inferences are patterns or trends that the researcher characterizes with simple narrative phrases and are distinct from the data described in the other columns. After the researcher has a chance to observe and reflect on the data sets, they can take a stab at generating a new insight that bridges the data sets.

Table 6.3 includes part of a joint display to illustrate the side-by-side column arrangement of key findings. The table reflects the mixed methods study by McLean et al. (2022), which was a convergent design to study web-based prolonged exposure therapy (Web-PE) to treat patients with posttraumatic stress disorder. Twenty-nine participants completed surveys and interviews on their experience. The researchers aimed to show the relationships among the key qualitative themes, exemplar quotes, relevant quantitative data, and their interpretations. Although the figure reflects that a small percentage of participants did not find the treatment to be helpful, the larger meta-inference is that the therapy was helpful.

Side-by-side joint displays can also include visual artifacts, such as photographs or maps, in a column. For example, Peroff et al. (2020) provided three side-by-side joint displays with photographs. Each joint display was labeled as to the overall content (e.g., "Photo Joint Display Illustrating Maya Attachment to Maize," p. 389). The first column included a photograph and the mean participant ranking of that photograph. These photographs and their rankings were paired with participant quotes (Column 2) and meta-inferences (Column 3).

Design Questions: As you design a side-by-side joint display, ask yourself the following questions:

• Which quantitative data can be listed in a column (Column 1 or 2, depending on the design)? Quantitative data reporting options include means, scores, effect sizes of score increases/decreases, factors, and percentages.

TABLE 6.3. Mixed Methods Results Table

Key qualitative themes (*n* = 28% reported)	Illustrative quotes	Relevant quantitative data	Mixed methods interpretation or meta-inference
Helpfulness (100%) **Definitely helpful** (77%)	"I think it was very helpful. Listening to the recording it got easier and easier the more I did it. It helped me process the memory and made me realize I was OK."	PWPQ (*n* = 29): 76%: Web-PE helped me better understand what I've been experiencing.	Web-PE was helpful in reducing PTSD symptoms for most participants. Participants felt that Web-PE helped them reflect and gain insight and that completing Web-PE was beneficial.
Somewhat helpful (14%)	"I benefited a little. Usually I always avoided, sb having to talk and think about it and confront it in a way I never did before helped me to actually deal with it."	69%: Web-PE improved my mental health. 76%: Web-PE asked me good questions that made me think.	
Not helpful (7%)	"I don't think online treatment for PTSD is a good idea. You can't have one treatment that will work well for everyone."	PCL-5 (*n* = 31): 64%: 10-point reduction. 45%: 20-point reduction.	

Note. PWPQ = Perceptions of Web-PE Questionnaire; PCL-5 = PTSD Checklist for *DSM-5*. Data from McLean et al. (2022).

- Which qualitative data can be listed in a column (Column 1 or 2, depending on the design)? Qualitative data reporting options include themes or categories, codes, and exemplar quotes.

- Which artifact data can be included (if appropriate), and should they be in a separate column or included in Column 1 or 2? Artifact data reporting options include maps, drawings, photographs, and charts (e.g., seating, organizational).

- What is the main meta-inference or mixed methods interpretation bridging the data sets (Column 3)? Meta-inference reporting options include summary phrases characterizing similarities or differences across data.

Option 2: Number-Coded and Color-Coded Joint Displays

Number-coded and color-coded joint displays use numbers, symbols, or colors to match qualitative and quantitative results in new ways. For example, quotes can be given the same color as a boxplot or other displays of quantitative results. Color can be useful with your team, great for conference presentations, and possible for publication purposes—that depends on the journal requirements.

Figure 6.2 shows a number-coded joint display that originally used color to visually represent the integration of qualitative and quantitative data implied in the mixed methods research question

> How do the quantitative and qualitative sets of results develop a more complete picture of vicarious posttraumatic growth in labor and delivery nurses who cared for women during traumatic births? (Beck et al., 2016, p. 805)

In their paper, Beck et al. (2016) provided a table with scores (on Posttraumatic Growth Inventory and Core Beliefs Inventory). Then, they described select interview themes. Their joint display includes a representative interview quote that exemplifies key concepts in each quantitative subscale. For example, the subscale Relating to Others (colored green in the original publication) is paired with a corresponding quote (also colored green):

> It takes more than one brain and two hands to be a L&D [labor and delivery] nurse. You need colleagues. You need them to let you cry out all the junk you accumulate when things go bad. I've changed because I've realized that teamwork is what makes me a better nurse and person. (p. 809)

In Figure 6.2, the colors were transformed into numbers to show the correspondence of the qualitative interview data and the quantitative data.

These data could have easily been represented in a table format, but it's arguably more striking and authentic to the raw data to preserve the box plot and associate the quotes by simply coloring them to match each box. This approach could be adapted for use with other types of quantitative data displays. The tricky part of using various quantitative displays is that they have little room to include quotes. A dilemma about presenting qualitative quotes is that they take up a lot of space. Therefore, it can be hard to decide how long the quote will be. It's best to be as judicious and parsimonious as possible with quote selection in a joint display. Use longer quotes in the narrative section of the article or consider a longer appendix showing the code table or a link to the raw data.

FIGURE 6.2. Number-Coded Joint Display

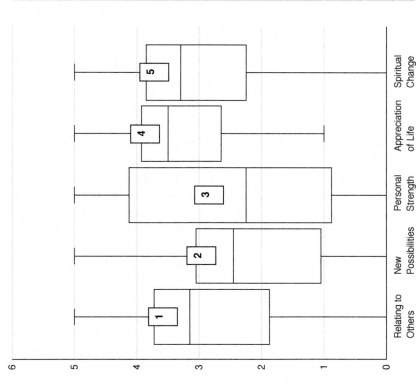

1. **Relating to others:** "It takes more than 1 brain and 2 hands to be a L & D [labor and delivery] nurse. You need colleagues. You need them to let you cry out all the junk you accumulate when things go bad. I've changed because I've realized that teamwork is what makes me a better nurse and person."

2. **New possibilities:** "My impetus for graduate education was in part from my experience caring for women with traumatic birth/outcomes."

3. **Personal strength:** "All the traumatic births have been points of growth for me. They have challenged me to grow as a RN, and given me valuable tools to use when encountering future difficult situations both personal and professional."

4. **Appreciation of life:** "It made me realize how precious life is and how quickly that can all be taken away. Through all this I have become more protective over my children and their safety as well as my own as I have a long commute after working night shifts that daily puts me in danger just being on the road."

5. **Spiritual change:** "My faith in God has grown over the years as I realize I have experienced and cared for patient cases others will never fathom to even imagine."

Note. Adapted from "Vicarious Posttraumatic Growth in Labor and Delivery Nurses," by C. T. Beck, C. M. Eaton, and R. K. Gable, 2016, *Journal of Obstetric, Gynecologic, and Neonatal Nursing, 45*(6), p. 809 (https://doi.org/10.1016/j.jogn.2016.07.008). Copyright 2016 by Elsevier. Adapted with permission.

Design Questions: As you design a number-coded or color-coded joint display, ask yourself the following questions:

- What qualitative and quantitative data can be colored to show similarities across the data?
- Which type of graphic display lends itself best to color?

Option 3: Creative Joint Displays

Creative joint displays use novel ways, other than tables or conventional diagrams, to tie the statistical results and corresponding thematic results to theories. Creative joint displays are rare and take the most ingenuity because the researchers must present the data in new ways without compromising the integrity of the results or the audience interpretation of them.

Figure 6.3 represents a creative joint display using concentric circles. Like the second joint display option, which provides numbers to relate the quantitative and qualitative data, these data could easily have been displayed as a table. However, Bustamante (2019) chose a series of concentric circles that link the theory with the data sets. This approach departs from most joint displays that report results only, without the theory. Although Bustamante used color (black to represent quantitative results, white to represent qualitative results, and gray to represent the discordance across the sets of results), it is the concentric circles that provide an innovation in joint display design. The innermost (first) circle depicts the main elements of TPACK (technical, pedagogical, and content knowledge) using three overlapping black circles, and it includes the significance levels. This type of Venn diagram is commonly used with TPACK theory. Bustamante chose to use the TPACK theory to guide the mixed methods data analysis as represented in the additional circles. The second circle (quantitative) shows the subscales used in the (quantitative) survey, including the significance values that correspond to the growth in each theoretical area, with significant results in black and nonsignificant results in grays. The third circle (qualitative) indicates the name of each interview them. Example themes are "Pedagogy behind technology," "Learning with web 2.0," and "Giving choices to students." No shading was used in this circle. The fourth circle (qualitative) provides the exemplar quotes (qualitative) that correspond to each theme. The shaded area represents a lack of congruency, both qualitatively and quantitatively: Quotes represent negative experiences and nonsignificant or significant results indicating no growth from baseline

FIGURE 6.3. Creative Joint Display

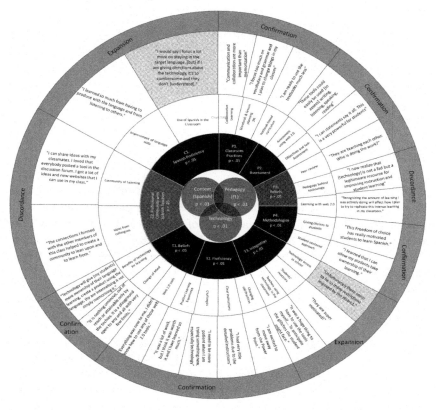

Note. From "TPACK and Teachers of Spanish: Development of a Theory-Based Joint Display in a Mixed Methods Research Case Study," by C. Bustamante, 2019, *Journal of Mixed Methods Research*, *13*(2), p. 171 (https://doi.org/10.1177/1558689817712119). Copyright 2019 by SAGE. Reprinted with permission.

measures. The fifth (outermost) circle (mixing of quantitative and qualitative) denotes the type of integration or mixing of the quantitative and qualitative data: confirmation (five areas), discordance (two areas), and expansion (two areas).

Creative joint displays might be less obvious to the reader and thus require careful explanation with a key, when appropriate. Ultimately, creative joint displays are very exciting when used to reimagine data and their relationships.

Design Question: As you design a creative joint display, ask yourself the following questions:

- If a traditional table or figure does not suffice for representing your mixed methods results, which shape(s) show the overlap or divergence of the qualitative and quantitative results?

- What kind of key and narrative explanation is necessary for explaining the joint display?

SUMMARY

Chapter 6 included discussion of the importance of methodological integrity, seven mixed methods validity strategies, and information about how each validity strategy fits with each type of mixed methods design. As your mixed methods project changes—depending on factors such as positionality, data collection availability and access, research partner needs, or dissertation committee requirements—it will likely be necessary to revisit validity and reliability as they correspond to selected measures and protocols. The chapter also included discussion of integration during sampling, data collection, data analysis, and reporting results. Finally, the chapter showed that side-by-side tables, color-coded joint displays, and creative joint displays are often creative and inventive ways display your mixed methods results. These displays do not replace individual tables and narrative explanations of the results, but they offer new insight that will likely stick in your audience's memory of your study when presented or published. Speaking of publishing, let's look at writing conventions in Chapter 7.

7 PRESENTING, WRITING, AND PUBLISHING MIXED METHODS RESEARCH

Congratulations! You're ready to get the word out about your mixed methods project. Maybe you're on the verge of completing your thesis, dissertation, or project, or you've got a conference presentation accepted. Whatever the reason, it's time to take the plunge into presenting, writing, and publishing. This chapter gives you tips on leaning into these opportunities. It also includes some tips for taking stock of what you've learned during the research process so you can share this experiential knowledge, in addition to your project results, with others.

This chapter helps you strategize and plan for getting your mixed methods project into tip-top shape and to meet the article reporting standards for mixed methods research (American Psychological Association [APA], 2020). Presenting, writing, and publishing don't necessarily happen in that sequence, but this chapter shows you how to leverage all your hard work so other people can learn about it (plus you can put it on your curriculum vitae). Publication is a requirement for academics, and there are other reasons for publication: You can help people learn about new research and help those interested in learning about mixed methods research learn

https://doi.org/10.1037/0000404-008
How to Mix Methods: A Guide to Sequential, Convergent, and Experimental Research Designs, by J. Katz-Buonincontro

about new methodological innovations that are part of your project. Who knows, you might come across a journal editor looking for manuscript submissions for a special issue when presenting at a conference, you might find a new collaborator or research group, or you might attract a new grant funder. The world is your presenting, writing, and publication oyster!

As you contemplate writing up and publishing your mixed methods project, you'll probably need to first present the project for internal team or committee purposes in addition to planning to present at conferences. This chapter includes three writing tips to help you explore the different options for organizing the Results section. Building on Chapter 6, this chapter also presents some ways in which authors address integration of the two (or more) sets of mixed methods results by using language to show how they compare to each other. Three publishing tips are presented to help you find a good fit between your research paper and potential publishing venues. Chapter 7 also introduces professional associations that showcase mixed methods research so you can deepen your knowledge and practice through membership, attending webinars, or pursuing a certificate or degree in mixed methods research.

PRESENTING

Connect with new audiences by presenting your mixed methods research. There are so many good reasons to start presenting different phases and aspects of a research project, especially before it's published! Presentation strategies vary and depend on the goal, audience, format, and type of presentation (e.g., paper session, poster session, roundtable, lightning session). In addition, it's possible to present the mixed methods framework that bridges the data sets before all the data are collected and analyzed.

Presenting Strategy 1: Convert Your Committee, Team, and Research Partners Into Your Champions

Convert your colleagues or professors into your research champions through presenting. Start small. Think of presenting as a way of communicating with your most important stakeholders: your committee members, collaborators, team members, students, supervisors, or research partners. Presenting is especially important for students and for early career academics who are reviewed annually and for mid-tenure, tenure, and promotion purposes.

Meetings with your stakeholders offer great opportunities to prepare and organize your thoughts and to present key status updates about your project. Depending on your audience, your presentation might not need to be perfectly polished. Use formal and informal meetings to announce news, such as recruitment and data collection milestones, to your teams, advisory board, or committee. When meeting with your team, entertain questions and engage in dialogue—presentations will help you get feedback to make the next presentation even stronger. It's okay to have setbacks, so let your team or professor know about them. The meeting process helps you work out any kinks and layer in any missing details. If you are the principal investigator, you might offer team members the opportunity to take turns presenting different aspects of the work, such as the context, the positionality statements, the design, the data collection, and the results. Don't have a meeting set up? Reach out and plan one! As discussed in Chapter 1, celebrate your teamwork as you make progress on your research, not just at the end.

As you prepare a meeting presentation,

- show how you meet the requirements of a thesis, dissertation, or prospective grant funder;
- share notes or slides, if appropriate, to model teamwork; and
- give credit to team members or committee members and use citations in the slides.

Presenting Strategy 2: Tap Into University, Local, and Regional Conferences

Give your mixed methods project visibility at conferences; academics are encouraged to present at prestigious disciplinary conferences. However, don't neglect the importance of presenting to your colleagues, especially in your department, college, or university. Pitches and competitions are opportunities to describe a research project. If you're a faculty member, postdoctoral fellow, or senior graduate student supervising a student, these opportunities provide students with an excellent chance to practice presenting in preparation for a disciplinary conference. Presentations showcase the mixed methods project as well as the student mentorship process across undergraduate and graduate students and faculty members. Presentations also highlight any interdisciplinary research collaborations across colleges within one university. Administrators like to see how collaborations are formed and how the collaborations benefit multiple groups of students and faculty members to strengthen the research enterprise, especially if the collaborations derive from internal grant funding.

Local conferences are also great for getting the word out about your research. If your mixed methods research project involves community partners or collaborations with nearby schools and colleges, then these conferences can offer fun opportunities for your team to connect with each other. Costs for local and regional conferences in a drivable radius are relatively negligible or minimal compared to national conferences. Typically, local conferences have special annual themes meant to advance the shared work of several groups and to make a local or regional impact, which means your presentation should be geared to that specific theme. Considering the complicated terminology used in mixed methods scholarship, you may need to adjust the use of technical terms. Also, because regional conferences might emphasize topical and trending issues in institutions (e.g., schools, museums, health organizations, government agencies, foundations, religious organizations, community organizations), think about how you are using your mixed methods design to address an issue in a unique way, compared to how others have used research to address the issue.

As you plan for presenting at a local/regional, or national/international conference,

- use language and tone appropriate to the audience. Layperson terms can explain and complement technical research terms used in mixed methods.

- address the special theme of the conference. Show how your mixed methods project uses both quantitative and qualitative research to address the special theme in a new way.

- initiate research conversations. When talking about your mixed methods project, seek ways to improve it as well as to improve the way you communicate the project to other researchers.

Presenting Strategy 3: Present at National and International Disciplinary Conferences

National and international research conferences are excellent opportunities to see what researchers are doing at other universities and learn from their work. Conferences are especially important when you are researching a niche area—you can connect with other researchers to share the latest cutting-edge research, especially in understudied areas. It's exciting to be part of small movements to generate new discovery on a topic, and conferences can be great sources of information that helps you to sharpen your technical expertise based on feedback you may receive. Sometimes travel grants can defray the cost to register and attend conferences, and sometimes conferences offer remote presentation opportunities.

It is often harder to get a research proposal accepted at national and international disciplinary conferences for several reasons. First, the selection criteria are often more rigorous in terms of the research design and often require the completion of data collection and analysis, as opposed to presenting on the design, plan and collaborative process of the mixed methods project (which are more appropriate for Strategies 1 and 2). Second, a greater number of proposals are submitted, making these conferences more competitive than other types of conferences. For these reasons, it's important to be clear and exacting when describing the phases of a mixed methods project in national and international conference proposals. The program chair and the program review committee may not be familiar with both qualitative and quantitative methods. Therefore, explain the mixed methods design and the type of quantitative and qualitative data when submitting a proposal.

It's also important to explain the project clearly when presenting. Consider beginning with a slide that has an overall diagram or graphic that shows the mixed methods project in its entirety, before breaking the project down into its parts. If your time is very limited, it's okay to focus on one main result or a joint display (see Chapter 6). You can refer conference attendees to a paper or website that includes all the qualitative and quantitative results if you are not able to present on them.

Eye-catching graphics are essential for a strong presentation, but clip art and many canned graphics are often not culturally sensitive. The concepts of research and science are often associated with visuals such as White men in lab coats, leading to the appearance that research communities are exclusive. Therefore, try to create your own graphics or use photographs and pictures that are truly representative of the people, places, and issues in your research. To ensure your graphics are interpreted accurately to the theme of your research and do not denote bias, practice presenting with your team and show your slide set or notes to your professor(s). If you anticipate using a photograph of study participants, you should be sure to request video or photograph permissions in your consent form when submitting or amending your human subjects protocol application. Remember to use permission when needed and cite references. Incorporating effective presentation of tables and figures can be accomplished by referencing books such as *Displaying Your Findings* (Nicol & Pexman, 2010a) and *Presenting Your Findings* (Nicol & Pexman, 2010b).

When presenting at a conference, researchers often don't get enough time to explain all phases of data collection, analysis, and results of a single-study project, let alone a comparatively larger mixed methods project. For example, you may get anywhere between 5 and 12 minutes of presentation time, so the onus is on the presenter to be as concise as possible. If the first presenter in a session takes more than their allotted time, the next presenters might get even less time than expected. If you are in this situation, let the audience know of a resource to find out more about your project, and be gracious to the other presenters.

As you strategize how to design a presentation on a mixed methods project at a large national or international research conference,

- provide a graphic showing the mixed methods project design before describing the data, and present a joint display if time allows;

- prioritize presenting key results, considering time constraints; and

- use culturally sensitive graphics that do not show bias and are representative of the people engaged in or participating in the project so as not to compromise the validity of the project context.

WRITING STRATEGIES

Writing up a paper, thesis, dissertation, or manuscript can feel overwhelming, especially with mixed methods projects. Demonstrating sufficient integration in the Results section is pinpointed as one of the most daunting parts of the writing process, especially when you are writing for high stakes (e.g., dissertation committee, blind peer review, grant review committee). Assume that your audience does not have much background in mixed methods research. The following writing strategies will help you be as clear and organized as possible to get published.

Writing Strategy 1: Write Early, Often, and in Your Own Words

It's not necessary to wait until the end of data collection and analysis to begin to write up a research report. Get your ideas on paper as soon as you think of them. Because mixed methods designs can take time to crystallize, try sketching the design on paper, a whiteboard, tablet, or computer. Take notes on mixed methods articles you read: Literature reviews and descriptions of your measures and protocols can be written up well before data collection is finished. You can use the descriptions you wrote for the human subjects protocol application and submitted to get permission to conduct research from your institution. When you begin collecting data, take notes. Field researchers often carry notebooks to record thoughts as they pop into their head—these notes are sometimes called memos—and to make notations for improving the quality of data collection and analysis.

Using a simple outline helps you to organize your work, to flesh out each section of your draft, and to see visual progress as you go. Frame the sample, context, data collection, and data analysis procedures and then review the details to make sure the chronology of events, sample size, and characteristics match the actual data collection procedures. These strategies help you to preserve the validity of data collection and analysis. When working with a team, these brief outlines and drafts help teams make progress and move forward. And lastly, if you are accountable to a committee or group of stake-holders, sharing outlines shows your progress and opens you up to feedback, which helps to reduce errors.

Use your own words to describe your research. Steer away from self-plagiarism or potential plagiarism of others by citing appropriately using the professional standards appropriate for the discipline (see APA, 2020). Further-more, the practice of writing helps you develop your own scholarly voice. Not all methodologists write the same. Some are very technical, whereas others prefer to integrate their reflections on research practice into their writing. For some examples, refer to the positionality statements in Chapter 1.

Tips for starting and maintaining a strong writing practice include

- write early, before data are collected and analyzed;

- write often—sketch ideas as they arise to help crystallize your mixed methods design, using a field notebook or the notes feature in your pre-ferred writing software or writing app; and

- write in your own words to preserve the validity of the order in which data are collected and to cultivate your own scholarly voice.

Writing Strategy 2: Use Strategic Mentoring for Writing

The collaborative nature of research also applies to writing. Try rotating the phases of presenting, writing, and publishing across your mixed methods team members to help distribute tasks and take the weight off one writer. If you have a team of students and researchers, you can try to match tasks to the skills people prefer as well as skills people want to develop. For example, some people shine at presenting and cringe at writing up research. Being good at one skill but not the other skill might seem like a limitation, but you can use these preferences to your advantage by focusing on your goal, which is to disseminate the results of the mixed methods research project.

When possible, let the person who likes to present or needs to get experience presenting take the lead in the presentation. If that star presenter needs practice writing, use strategic mentoring to improve their writing. The experienced writers on the team can swap leadership roles with the presenter. That is, they can take the lead and serve as writing mentors to a team member who prefers presenting.

Discuss authorship order, which may change as the manuscript progresses. As a team, you can discuss discipline-specific rules, such as those found in Section 1.22 of the *Publication Manual of the American Psychological Association* (7th ed.; APA, 2020). Some research labs or groups defer to the lead researcher or principal investigator (if a grant project) to initiate a discussion about the order of authorship, but the lead researcher is not necessarily the lead author: In some cases, students are listed first, and the principal investigator is listed last. If a research team has more than one publication opportunity, the order of authors might rotate, depending on the amount of work each person contributed. Another option is to draft an author's note stating equal authorship.

When working on a specific writing opportunity, it's possible to divide the writing tasks based on each team member's expertise and interests. For example, one writer can draft the literature review while another writer can draft the methods, recruitment, and sample descriptions. Within the literature review, one section might speak to a team member's own research agenda, while another section might relate to another team member's dissertation research, for example. If that's the case, divide the sections according to each writer's familiarity with the content and burgeoning expertise. The final phase of writing can involve editing the piece to ensure a unified writing voice.

Perhaps most relevant to experienced mixed methods teams, each team member can take ownership for a specific methodological area within the larger mixed methods project. For example, a qualitative researcher might write the qualitative method section, describe the interview design, note relevant methodological citations, and compose the qualitative interview results section. The quantitative researcher could do the same for the quantitative methods, planned analyses, and the quantitative results section. The team leader could write the mixed methods description and the mixed methods integrated results section and could review the other sections for completeness and a unified writing voice.

To summarize, ways to be strategic about mentoring for writing include

• Matching writing opportunities to team members' skills, preferences, and developmental needs

- Dividing writing tasks according to each team members' content expertise

- Fostering ownership of writing methodological sections within the larger mixed methods project (e.g., qualitative, quantitative, mixed methods sections)

- Being flexible, fair, and generous about authorship and author order, using the guidelines set by the discipline. You may refer to the guidelines provided by APA (2020, Section 1.22).

Writing Strategy 3: Select a Way to Organize Your Results

There are so many options, conventions, and published examples for writing Results sections for mixed methods projects. To start, the first writing principle to follow is analytic comprehensiveness. Make sure to include all the data, especially if you have multiple phases in a mixed methods research project. Jot down a short outline or list of the data. That way, you'll be sure not to accidentally skip any results.

If you've already mastered the skill of writing a Results section for a mixed methods project, consider how to fine-tune the presentation of the results. Tell the reader whether the mixed methods projects accord priority or equal status to the qualitative and quantitative sections. Priority status means a specific type of data is the predominant focus of the project, emphasized in the data collection, analysis, and results.

Balance a Qualitative Results Section With a Quantitative Results Section

Follow the project's mixed methods design: Be conscientious about matching the results to the data collection procedures. For example, if you have an explanatory sequential design with quantitative methods followed by qualitative methods, then your Results section can mirror this data collection sequence: The Results section (first heading) may have a subsection titled Quantitative Results (second-level heading) followed by a subsection titled Qualitative Results (second-level heading). West et al. (2013) used this format in their study of nursing students. They presented their quantitative results in four subsections:

1) Student commencement members
2) Student progression rates
3) Student attrition rates
4) Student completion rates

For the qualitative results, the authors reported five themes of Indigenous nursing success:

1) Individual student characteristics
2) Academic knowledge, awareness, and understanding
3) Relationships, connections, and partnerships
4) Institutional structures, systems, and processes
5) Family and community knowledge, awareness, and understanding

The results were then compared across both these sections and the integration was presented in the Discussion section. In this study, the comparison of quantitative results and qualitative results showed, among other things, a lack of institutional tactics to address a shortage of Indigenous nurses and that Indigenous nursing students cited peer networks to mitigate racism and cultural isolation.

Alternatively, you can include a third section, Mixed Methods Results (second-level heading), that bridges the data sets. For example, if your project has multiple data sets, you might have a section titled Qualitative Results (second-level heading) with subsections (third-level headings) such as Interview Themes and Observation Data, followed by a section titled Quantitative Results (second-level heading) with subsections for each type of analysis (third-level headings), and final a section titled Mixed Methods (second-level heading).

One mistake that some authors make when writing about their study is to overstate their data or reference data that were not analyzed. For example, if a project included interviews and ethnographic observations but the write-up reports only the interview results, then the internal validity seems compromised. To uphold the principles of transparency, integrity, and openness, be consistent in the results you report. If you wanted to conduct observations initially but did not end up obtaining access, then state that in the Procedures section. Reporting only one of two stated data sets leads to confusion or possible misrepresentation of data.

Writing Up Themes

Integrating the qualitative and quantitative results by theme is also an appropriate way to write up results. For example, Cooper and Hall (2016) integrated the qualitative and quantitative phases of their convergent mixed methods study by presenting three themes. This writing strategy shows the researchers' meta-inferences concerning both qualitative and quantitative data. For instance, "a nurturing familial environment" was written up as a theme (p. 56), supported by quotes from interviews and focus groups. To complement these data, Cooper and Hall reported survey results and correlations between students' self-rated academic and social experiences.

Writing Up Cases Using a Culturally Relevant Framework

Case selection options vary depending on the most salient points the researchers aim to direct the reader's attention to. For example, cases can be organized by geographical region, organizational type, or psychological orientation. They can also be organized using a culturally relevant approach, revealing that the most important aspect of the results is the emic, or insider, understanding of cultural norms and ways of acting through observation, communication, and other data collection methods.

For example, Hatta et al. (2020) used two ways to organize their results: a case methodology approach (cf. Onwuegbuzie et al., 2010) and a culturally relevant framework. They selected cases from a larger study to examine oncologists' and cancer patients' dialogues and diagnosis processes. Interchanges between oncologist and patient were interpreted according to a rhetorical framework of ki-shou-ten-ketsu, used in the Japanese language (Hinds, 1980, as cited in Hatta et al., 2020). In the following passage from the article, "Ki" represents the first stage of discussion, which is the introduction of the topic, and highlights the concept of omakase, or an entrusting dynamic between patient and doctor:

> *Introduction (Ki) for Case No29, a Patient with Breast Cancer that Illustrates the Omakase (Entrusting) Approach.*

In contrast to this case, patients with low motivation seemed somewhat vulnerable or passive at the beginning of the informed consent consultation, as below:

DR [DOCTOR]:	Where shall we start?
PT [PATIENT]:	My husband has already retired and stays at home, and he was saying that he was going to listen to the discussion with me, but today he has to look after my grandchild, so he told me to go and listen so that I understand everything (laughs).
DR:	There are lots of things to talk about, so it's better that your husband does come eventually. I don't think you can cope with (1.0 s pause) this treatment all alone.
PT:	Sorry. (Hatta et al., p. 98)

In this case study, the patient–doctor conversation was organized according to Ki, the first stage of discussion, using a Japanese cultural framework. This excerpt shows how the doctor deferred to the patient to open up, talk, and disclose information and hence built trust to treat the patient.

To summarize, you can organize your results by case, deciding on the salient points to highlight such as using a culturally relevant interpretation and deciding which qualitative or quantitative data supports evidence of this culturally relevant interpretation. The first-level header might be "Description of Cultural Values, Principles, or Customs," and the second-level headers might introduce example dialogue, quotes, observations, or self-reported ratings.

Writing Up a Typology

Showcasing a typology of beliefs, ideologies, perspectives, or pedagogies is another way to write up the quantitative and qualitative results in a mixed methods research project. Typologies show a range of different thoughts or ways of doing something. They might include statistical results from surveys coupled with verbal descriptions from interviews, for example. In one mixed methods study, for example, Stolz (2017) described four belief types concerning God, pulled from survey data and interview data in Switzerland: institutional, alternative, distanced, and secular beliefs. Stolz described each belief type and included the percentage of participants of each type and then contextualized the explanations with the interview data. Stolz described select individuals to help explain certain enigmas in the data about religiosity and spirituality. For example, the quantitative data showed a relatively high age for conversion in Evangelical Christianity compared to other religions, which did not make sense until the interviews revealed the age at which people attended a conversion camp.

You could organize your results by typology and then compare them at the end:

Type 1 "Description"

  Quantitative results

  Qualitative results

Type 2 "Description"

  Quantitative results

  Qualitative results

Comparison of typologies

WRITING MIXED METHODS GRANT PROPOSALS

Planning and writing a grant proposal differs from writing a manuscript, but how? Mixed methods grant proposals are more constrained than mixed methods theses, dissertations, or studies because they need to meet criteria set by the funding organization. Federal agencies, nonprofit organizations, and professional associations offer grants to support their missions and strategic plans (Wisdom & Fetters, 2015). Therefore, mixed methods grant proposals need to fit into the scope, aims, and related parameters of grant programs.

Because most large grants require an internal or an external evaluation of the project, many grant evaluators use basic mixed methods designs. For example, evaluators might survey the people who benefit from a project that introduces a new technological innovation or intervention, and they might also include multiple focus groups to get feedback on the technology or intervention.

Sometimes research competitions offer funding pitches in rounds. For example, you might be asked first to submit just an initial proposal or topic. If the review committee selects your proposal in this first round of review, they may invite you to present a project overview, to be reviewed for potential funding. If that's the case, use the grant research funding proposal criteria as major headings in your proposal to show how you are addressing basic requirements. Applicants almost always include a Gantt chart to show each task by year, including which team member works in each area. Such charts help to establish a justification for the budget and shows the alignment between type of task and type of expertise.

Some common pitfalls of grant planning and writing include neglecting to look at the funding eligibility criteria, federally negotiated institutional overhead rates (the amount allotted to the college or university), and other important details such as fringe rates. Some grants require matching funds and stipulate what they will and will not fund. Focus on the essential costs to get the research done: personnel. To that end, try to stretch the grant opportunity to mentor postdoctoral scholars and students. On a mixed methods team, each researcher might mentor a student in their specific methodological area. Working in a team allows for wonderful debate about the best methods to use in each part of the mixed methods project and allows students to learn from each other, and faculty to learn from students, too! Therefore, including a student or postdoctoral fellow on a mixed methods grant proposal can advance mentoring in mixed methods in your specific area or field.

As you plan for writing a mixed methods grant,

- Get a good understanding of the funding world in your project area. Work with your foundations office, corporate relations office, or institutional advancement office.

- Talk with your director, department chair, or associate dean to champion your idea to funding prospects.

- Make a database of possible funders, including philanthropic organizations, federal agencies (National Education Association [NEA], U.S. National Science Foundation [NSF], National Institutes of Health [NIH], the Institute of Education Sciences [IES], U.S. Department of Education), state agencies, and city agencies.

- Make a grant application calendar to help stay on track and to ensure you do not miss new opportunities debuted by funders, who may not be required to publish application criteria more than 60 days prior to the application due date.

PUBLISHING

Publishing strategies can depend on your dissertation requirements, career goals, field, and potential fit with journal scope and aims. Some journals explicitly focus on mixed methods, making it possible for you to publish every data set together in one manuscript. On the other hand, discipline- or field-based journals that prioritize the contribution to theory and research in a particular field may not be as concerned with the technical details for reporting mixed methods. This section of the chapter provides tips for parsing large mixed methods projects into separate manuscripts while avoiding piecemeal publication (e.g., Section 1.16 in the *Publication Manual* [APA, 2020]). Though this task may seem daunting at first blush, there's helpful advice out there, including the journal article reporting standards for mixed methods. (APA, 2020, pp. 106–108)

Publishing Strategy 1: Publish a Literature Review From a Thesis or Dissertation

A synthesis of past studies in an area, originally written to ground a larger project such as a dissertation or grant, can be published as an expanded, stand-alone literature review or synthesis. As covered in Chapter 2, literature syntheses can help readers understand the state of a field and think about gaps or deficiencies. These syntheses can highlight methodological discrepancies of single-method articles in a certain area and point toward the need for mixed methods research. Researchers often enjoy reading and citing literature syntheses because their authors have already done the work to find and summarize research in the area of interest. For more on this topic, you may want to consult *Using Mixed Methods Research Synthesis for Literature Reviews* (Heyvaert et al., 2017).

Some key points about publishing literature syntheses from a mixed methods project include

- Use appropriate search terms and search term combinations to generate relevant articles for the synthesis.
- Describe search parameters, dates, and clear inclusion and exclusion criteria.
- Provide a framework for reviewing, synthesizing, and analyzing the literature.
- Outline clear gaps in past studies.
- Show how mixed methods might be able to address the stated gaps.

Publishing Strategy 2: Publish in a Disciplinary Journal

If you are aiming to advance a particular field, it's important to publish in discipline-specific journals. The drawback of disciplinary journals is that the word count limitation often does not allow for a full description of all the data sets used in a mixed methods project. As a result, some mixed methods projects are simplified and condensed when published in a journal article. This issue can present a real challenge, especially when the researcher is aiming to provide contextualized accounts of both quantitative and qualitative data. Because the allowable word count in discipline-specific journals is sometimes relatively low, mixed methods researchers may need to simplify and condense their projects for publication, and you might read shortened versions of the actual mixed methods project in journals.

When facing the dilemma of how to publish your mixed methods study, it can be helpful to consider publishing a short version or part of the study in a disciplinary journal first. Disciplinary journal editors are looking for ways that your study advances the field and extends theory and practice in certain areas. In addition, journal editors are often concerned with how the manuscript speaks to the journal readership, which might be international, country specific, or very niche oriented in terms of addressing mostly practitioners, scholars, or a blend of scholar–practitioners. It might be helpful to show the lineage of articles published on your topic in that specific journal. As a complementary publishing strategy, you could seek to publish more elaborated discussion about aspects of the study and the method in a mixed methods journal. Publishing in a journal is like a conversation frozen in time. You are aiming to publish an article, but that article is interpreted in the context of a field and in the context of that journal.

When publishing in a disciplinary journal, do your homework (see Appendix B):

- Read about the journal scope, aims, editorial board, and type of manuscripts.
- Identify mixed methods articles published in that journal.

- Review articles on your mixed methods topic by content area in that journal.
- Cite both methodological and content-related articles that hail from the journal you aim to publish in.

Publishing Strategy 3: Publish About an Innovation in Mixed Methods Research

Increasingly, journals are flexible about publishing mixed methods research in addition to quantitative and/or qualitative research. Depending on the journal, you can include descriptions of your experiential research knowledge, what you have learned in the field, to complement the technical write-up of the quantitative and qualitative data.

Appendix B lists some journals that specifically aim to publish mixed methods research. There is precedent for publishing mixed methods studies in journals published by the APA as well as in journals from other fields. The premier mixed methods journal is the *Journal of Mixed Methods Research*, and a growing number of journals are publishing mixed methods in psychology and related fields. Publishing in a mixed methods journal requires you to find a journal that focuses on excellence in mixed methods design. Follow the 10 mixed methods design essentials presented in Chapter 2 and review the reflection questions to make sure you hit on all the elements. Make sure you follow the mixed methods journal article reporting standards (APA, 2020).

Researchers with experience in the field conducting mixed methods research and who have worked with different teams publish special innovations in mixed methods designs. As the field is relatively new, there are a lot of excellent articles explaining a specific type of mixed methods research using visual aids, the arts, dance therapy, case study, maps and geography, interventions, culturally specific research, and other important advances. Look for journals that publish special issues on methodological innovations to submit your own special innovation in mixed methods research and contemplate whether your innovation might warrant a full-length article explaining how it extends the field of mixed methods research.

Publishing on innovations in mixed methods research can require you to

- demonstrate mastery in standard mixed methods practices,

- detail the innovative aspects of your mixed methods design, and

- point out how the innovation extends past a traditional mixed methods design in a unique way that does not compromise rigor and validity standards.

PROFESSIONAL ASSOCIATIONS

Professional associations are large learning communities for supporting and exchanging ideas, sharing knowledge about the latest advancements in research methodology, and supporting professional development. They play a key role in shaping fields, especially research methods. Mixed methods researchers congregate and present their work across a variety of networks and professional associations. If you are able, consider joining an association, or start your own group in your program, research lab, college, or university.

American Psychological Association

APA's Division 5, Quantitative and Qualitative Methods (https://www.apadivisions.org/division-5/index), includes researchers who work in mixed methods. Its mission is stated as follows: "Div. 5 draws together specialists in the areas of quantitative and qualitative methods. Our membership includes specialists in the fields of educational psychology, industrial-organizational psychology, individual assessment, measurement, program evaluation, psychometrics, qualitative inquiry, research interviewing, research methods and statistics" (para. 1). Other APA divisions work in mixed methods as well. For example, Division 27, Community Psychology (https://scra27.org/who-we-are/mission/principles/), states, "Community research and action is an active collaboration among researchers, practitioners, and community members that uses multiple methodologies. Such research and action must be undertaken to serve those community members directly concerned, and should be guided by their needs and preferences, as well as by their active participation" (para. 1). Other divisions in which mixed methods might be relevant are Division 15: Educational Psychology and Division 8: Personality and Social Psychology.

American Educational Research Association

Another prominent professional organization that showcases work in mixed methods is the American Educational Research Association (AERA). AERA has a special interest group, Mixed Methods Research (158; https://www.aera.net/SIG158/Mixed-Methods-Research-SIG-158), with the mission "to support, encourage, and increase dialogue and idea exchange among educational researchers utilizing mixed methods and those interested in integrating qualitative and quantitative research approaches" (para. 1). AERA Division D, Measurement and Research Methodologies (https://www.aera.net/

Division-D/Measurement-Research-Methodologies-D), focuses on measurement, psychometrics and assessment; statistical theory and quantitative methodologies; qualitative methodologies; and multiple and mixed methodologies as applied to educational research.

Mixed Methods International Research Association

Mixed Methods International Research Association (MMIRA) is the premier mixed methods research association. They have the broadest reach across fields. For example, the MMIRA Global Conference is located in different cities around the world and has international chapters in the Caribbean and Japan. MMIRA also offers massive open online courses, sometimes called MOOCs, on mixed methods designs and student chapters.

Japan Society for Mixed Methods Research

This society specializes in mixed methods research as well: https://publichealth.jhu.edu/academics/academic-programs/training-grants/mixed-methods-research-training-program-for-the-health-sciences

Sociological and Health Science Organizations

Sociological organizations that encourage mixed methods research include the American Sociological Association, the International Sociological Association, the Sociologists for Women in Society, and the Comparative and International Education Society.

Research documenting outcomes in health sciences research also use mixed methods as evidenced by journals (e.g., *International Journal of Obesity*), as well as books, websites, and YouTube workshops such as one sponsored by the International Institute for Qualitative Methodology.

Federal Agencies

Federal agencies help shape scientific fields by supporting the use of different types of research methods to tackle problems in society and ensuring the rigor of these methods for open and transparent science for the public good. For example, the NSF, the IES, and the NIH refer explicitly to the use of mixed methods designs in grant proposals and indicate concern about the quality of mixed methods training in their respective fields. As evidenced in recent IES, NIH, and NSF web-based handbooks, mixed methods are gathering momentum to shape several fields of human science, health psychology, and education. One reason health science mixed methods research is important is that "Mixed methods also can speed translation from a tested intervention to evidence-based interventions in real-life settings that often have more complexities than the environments in which funded intervention research occurs" (Creswell et al., 2011, p. 3). In addition, researchers testified in a large report about the importance of mixed methods relative to their fields in education. For example, one researcher described revealing "hidden processes and individuals' decision-making strategies" (IES, 2015, p. 5).

UNIVERSITY-BASED MIXED METHODS CONFERENCES AND PROGRAMS

Several international and American universities have arranged miniconferences, workshops, certificates, training institutes, and programs featuring mixed methods precisely because of the widespread interest among faculty and students who desire more training in psychology, education, public health, medicine, and business/management. Appendix C includes a list of university programs specializing in mixed methods research.

SUMMARY

Chapter 7 caps off the research cycle of designing, conducting, and analyzing your mixed methods research project with tips to disseminate, share, and publish your work effectively. The chapter includes three presenting approaches, four writing tactics, and three publishing strategies. Though the publication phase brings mixed methods research into fruition for all to learn about, it also plants the seed for the next wave of research. New mixed methods research questions and hypotheses can be planned to counterbalance the inherent limitations of the project. The cycle of mixed methods research continues with new ideas in the continued quest to solve societal problems.

Tips for writing grant proposals are provided to enhance the realistic, painstaking, and rewarding process of planning and writing grant applications. Because many journals now accept manuscripts that describe mixed methods studies in addition to literature syntheses and single-study empirical research papers, the list of journals in Appendix B can help you weigh the pros and cons of various publication outlets and the appropriateness of your mixed methods study for disciplinary-oriented journals. In addition, the increasing array of mixed methods certificates, programs, and institutes, coupled with the widening representation of mixed methods research at major research conferences sponsored by professional organizations, shines a bright light on the future of the field of mixed methods research. Here's hoping that you will be excited to join and participate in the field!

CONCLUSION

Lumps aren't the enemy!

–Alyssa Jung and Lauren Chan

Let's return to the pancake batter analogy from the Introduction of this book. In the quote that introduces this Conclusion, the bakers Alyssa Jung and Lauren Chan are referring to the little lumps of flour that form when mixing batter. "Lumps" is a metaphor for the constant improvement and adjustment involved in designing and carrying out mixed methods projects when facing the messiness and imperfections of working in new areas. Eventually, lumps dissolve and work themselves out. Lumps result in the researcher producing a high-quality mixed methods project because they draw the researcher's attention to areas for clarification, adjustments, and improvement that hopefully make your mixed methods project better than when you started designing it.

In this book, you've had a chance to explore the major mixed methods designs (sequential, convergent, and experimental) and to learn about

https://doi.org/10.1037/0000404-009
How to Mix Methods: A Guide to Sequential, Convergent, and Experimental Research Designs, by J. Katz-Buonincontro

specialized "bespoke" designs that speak to a specific context (e.g., culturally specific designs; arts-based, case study, and physiological data-based experimental designs) without sacrificing rigor, quality, and integrity. In addition, you've been exposed to research concepts including integration, joint displays, mixed methods validity, and meta-inferences that are unique to the mixed methods field. Over time, these key mixed methods concepts arose as researchers drew on their experiences and tried new approaches in a variety of different fields. They have challenged themselves and each other to clarify, refine, and produce language to describe and unify the mixed methods field to help produce valid, reliable, and usable science. Mixed methods research evolves as it embraces research developments from other areas. For example, positionality and reflexivity practices, once used mostly in qualitative research, are becoming more widespread in mixed methods research and can help you reflect on ways to make your project the best it can be. The trends in replication and extension as well as openness and transparency, emphasized especially in quantitative methods, are important for producing rigorous mixed methods work. These mixed methods innovations will continue to have a positive impact on the social sciences because they help researchers to be clear and exacting when understanding and making sense out of data.

Like these researchers who have innovated and adapted mixed methods designs, you too can add your voice to the chorus of knowledge. Maybe, just maybe, your research self-efficacy—the belief that you are becoming a competent mixed methods researcher—is also developing and taking shape. As you build your methodological chops and develop your own unique scholarly voice, you'll naturally become more confident and develop new research skills and interests. You'll make some mistakes but learn from them and grow. It's my hope that you return to this book as a resource over the trajectory of your career as a student or academic researcher to design, plan, conduct and analyze projects and that you use it to think about an appropriate writing, presenting, publishing, or grant-writing strategy that reflects your project needs at the time.

Researchers, both seasoned and novice, are increasingly open to appreciating the qualities of both qualitative and quantitative research to see how they can be used in conjunction with one another. This methodological orientation departs from older ways of methods training, in which people stay in one lane, so to speak, and use the same research methods at the expense of being open to new ways of doing research. The field of mixed methods is helping advance the fields of social, educational, behavioral, and health sciences to be more open, diverse, and inclusive of different research strategies and of different research topics. With these innovations, academia is becoming more inclusive of globally, racially, ethnically, and gender diverse researchers who see themselves as part of the field and its future. We've come to learn that mixed methods researchers

- see the world as holding multiple truths, including feminist and culturally sensitive approaches;

- include both quantitative and qualitative data in the major mixed methods designs without compromising the validity and reliability standards associated with each individual method;

- balance scientific rigor with humanism;

- showcase the merging and integration of the quantitative and qualitative data sets;

- design creative, complex, and side-by-side joint displays;

- describe compelling takeaways that are useful in organizations, a field, and/or a set of theories;

- engage in reciprocal learning with team members; and

- open doors for others through stratified research mentoring and partnering with community members.

In the coming years, mixed methods research will continue to grow along these fronts:

- Methodological sophistication. The maturity of the mixed methods field can be discerned in the recent adoption and consistent use of mixed methods terminology such as sampling integration, joint displays, and meta-inferences. Over the past decade, these terms developed but were not discussed in every textbook or journal article. Now, however, they are commonplace. This terminology will continue to be adopted by students and professionals foraying into the field, who will help to build a common language.

- Professional acceptance. Mixed methods research is becoming normalized in research circles, especially those open to innovation. It's integrated into a variety of research groups and starting to appeal to young researchers, including those in high school and undergraduate programs. Professional organizations increasingly accept and feature mixed methods presentations at conferences, editors publish mixed methods in journals, and agencies and foundations fund mixed methods grants.

- Disciplinary diversification. With roots in areas such as program evaluation, mixed methods research approaches now span health, medicine, psychology, the arts, education, political science, geography, and business. Research mentoring has expanded to include mixed methods projects, with the spirit of learning and sharing methodological knowledge in the service of solving research problems that plague society. Increasingly, researchers are using or embedding mixed methods into larger projects, indicating a diversification of the field. Thus, a trend is making mixed methods more sensitive to contextual factors such as the progression of time, organizational needs, cultural relevance, and community input (Creswell, 2022).

- Technological embracement. Mixed methods researchers specializing in the use of technology combine qualitative and statistical software with other types of software to provide mixed methods analyses. For example, geotagging has been explored to pair visual images from Google Earth with quantitative variables and qualitative coding of text (Peladeau, 2021). With multiple streams of data afforded by social media, researchers are figuring out how best to pull and organize data, layer these data by case, and map out new theories based on the data (cf. Onwuegbuzie & Johnson, 2021). Another example is using social network analysis to measure the strength of associations between people, which can be further elaborated with qualitative interviews (Fetters, 2020). As our lives become more entwined with advances such as wearable technology, natural language processing (NLP), and artificial intelligence (AI), mixed methods research will continue to find innovative ways to highlight the affordances of technology for special mixed analyses, for example the use of conversational agents to augment behavioral change (Nadarzynski et al., 2019). Researchers increasingly use NLP to treat qualitative data in mixed methods research, for example conducting automated content analysis of text passages to estimate word frequencies (Reinhold et al., 2023). Some data analysis software packages provide an option to use AI to code text passages (e.g., https://www.intellectusstatistics.com/), and researchers also develop their own AI agents to assist with analysis of specialized qualitative expressions in rapid ways (Lennon et al., 2021).

Keep memos of trends like these, observe how they affect your research field, note controversies that might arise, and contemplate how your own mixed methods research studies might adopt new techniques and make headway on important issues. Most important, don't give up on mixed methods research as you design a study. Even if the study is not published, you can still contribute to your field. Mixed methods research practice takes grit (to propose and defend both quantitative and qualitative methodological integrity), resilience (to persist with a project in the face of study attrition, funding gaps, and insufficient time), patience (to work with interdisciplinary teams and collaborators), and creativity (to press forward, contribute new ideas, and solve big problems in society).

A fitting way to end this book is to ask you, the reader, what does your research future hold? How will you help people improve their lives and society with usable research? And, what exciting work will you contribute to help advance the field of mixed methods? As you make progress with your mixed methods research project, may you enjoy this journey and find much success!

Appendix A

MIXED METHODS DESIGNS AND MAJOR STEPS

Steps	Sequential		Convergent	Experimental
	Explanatory	Exploratory		
Step 1	**Start with the quantitative strand: The "what"**	**Start with the qualitative strand**	**Prioritize or equally weight the quantitative and qualitative strands**	**Design the experiment**
Description	Select type of quantitative data and analyses Select the main results for qualitative explanation	Develop qualitative interview or focus group questions get to the heart of genuine experiences, perspectives to then build (or revise) a new quantitative instrument	Order the research questions and hypotheses	Select the number, type, and duration of conditions, calculate the sample size and statistical power
Step 2	**Sequence the qualitative strand: The "why" or "how"**	**Sequence the quantitative strand**	**Capture co-occurrence through data collection**	**Use qualitative methods before, during, or after an intervention**
Description	Identify phenomena, lived experiences, thought patterns, or belief systems connecting to the quantitative items, factors, correlations, or predictions	Describe the qualitative themes for a quantitative instrument and pilot test the instrument	Identify co-occurring or nonlinear trajectories and events and decide if the sample will be the same in the quantitative and qualitative strands	Sample participants from the intervention to tailor the intervention to groups, to understand the intervention experience, or to debrief participants
Step 3	**Compare the quantitative and qualitative results**	**Compare the qualitative results to the quantitative results**	**Merge the quantitative and qualitative results**	**Merge the quantitative and qualitative results**
Description	Characterize the correspondence between the quantitative and qualitative results: Confirmatory, explanatory, convergent or divergent, discordant	Examine the adequacy of qualitative thematic representation in resulting survey or instrument and analyze the data from the new survey or instrument	Compare and explain how the results illuminate each other	Calculate intervention results by selecting appropriate statistical test and thematize narrative experiences from interviews

Note. Please refer to the chapters to see how each design can vary depending on the specific needs of the participants and context of the study as well as special features such as using physiological measures or arts-based activities.

Appendix B

JOURNALS THAT PUBLISH MIXED METHODS RESEARCH

Journal	Publisher
Mixed methods research (general)	
Journal of Mixed Methods Research https://journals.sagepub.com/home/mmr	Sage
Methods in Psychology https://www.sciencedirect.com/journal/methods-in-psychology	Science Direct
American Behavioral Scientist https://journals.sagepub.com/home/abs	Sage
General psychology	
Behavior Research Methods https://www.springer.com/journal/13428	Springer
Qualitative Psychology https://www.apa.org/pubs/journals/qua	APA
Frontiers in Psychology https://www.frontiersin.org/journals/psychology	Frontiers
Counseling and therapy	
Counselling Psychology Quarterly https://www.tandfonline.com/journals/ccpq20	Taylor & Francis Online
Clinical Psychology: Science and Practice, Developmental Psychology https://onlinelibrary.wiley.com/journal/14682850	Wiley
Journal of Marital and Family Therapy https://onlinelibrary.wiley.com/journal/17520606	Wiley
Psychiatric Services https://www.appi.org/psychiatric_services	American Psychiatric Association
Methods in Psychology https://www.sciencedirect.com/journal/methods-in-psychology	ScienceDirect
Journal of Theoretical and Philosophical Psychology https://www.apa.org/pubs/journals/teo	APA

(continues)

Journal	Publisher
Psychology of Violence https://www.apa.org/pubs/journals/vio	APA
Psychotherapy https://www.apa.org/pubs/journals/pst	APA
Nursing and health	
Journal of Research in Nursing https://journals.sagepub.com/home/jrn	Sage
Health and Social Care in the Community https://onlinelibrary.wiley.com/journal/13652524	Wiley
Qualitative Health Research https://journals.sagepub.com/home/qhr	Sage
Journal of Health Psychology https://journals.sagepub.com/home/hpq	Sage
Families, Systems, & Health https://www.apa.org/pubs/journals/fsh	APA
Journal of Counseling Psychology https://www.apa.org/pubs/journals/cou	APA
Annals of Family Medicine https://www.annfammed.org/	Annals of Medicine, Inc.
Family Medicine and Community Health https://fmch.bmj.com/	BMJ Journals
Health Services Research https://www.hsr.org/authors	Wiley
Journal of General Internal Medicine https://www.springer.com/journal/11606	Springer
Journal of Interpersonal Violence https://us.sagepub.com/en-us/nam/journal/journal-interpersonal-violence#submission-guidelines	Sage
Journal of Medical Internet Research https://link.springer.com/journal/11606	JMIR Publications
Social Science & Medicine https://www.sciencedirect.com/journal/social-science-and-medicine	ScienceDirect
Contemporary Nurse https://www.tandfonline.com/journals/rcnj20	Taylor & Francis Online
Education	
Educational Researcher https://journals.sagepub.com/home/edr	Sage
Teaching and Teacher Education https://www.sciencedirect.com/journal/teaching-and-teacher-education	ScienceDirect
Contemporary Educational Psychology https://www.sciencedirect.com/journal/contemporary-educational-psychology	ScienceDirect

Journal	Publisher
Educational Research and Evaluation https://www.tandfonline.com/journals/nere20	Taylor & Francis Group
American Journal of Evaluation https://journals.sagepub.com/home/aje	Sage
Journal of MultiDisciplinary Evaluation https://journals.sfu.ca/jmde/index.php/jmde_1	Western Michigan University, PKP Publishing Services
Frontiers in Education https://www.frontiersin.org/journals/education	Frontiers
Journal of Educational Administration https://www.emerald.com/insight/publication/issn/0957-8234	Emerald Publishing
Educational Evaluation and Policy Analysis https://journals.sagepub.com/home/epa	Sage
Psychology in the Schools https://onlinelibrary.wiley.com/journal/15206807	Wiley
Methodology	
Field Methods https://journals.sagepub.com/home/fmx	Sage
International Journal of Multiple Research Approaches https://www.tandfonline.com/toc/rmra20/current	Dialectical Publishing
International Journal of Qualitative Methods https://www.ualberta.ca/international-institute-for-qualitative-methodology/international-journal-of-qualitative-methods.html *[this journal also publishes MMR protocol papers]*	Sage
International Journal of Research & Method in Education https://www.tandfonline.com/journals/cwse20	Taylor & Francis Online
International Journal of Social Research Methodology https://www.tandfonline.com/journals/cwse20	Taylor & Francis Online
Qualitative Inquiry https://journals.sagepub.com/home/qix	Sage
Quality & Quantity https://www.springer.com/journal/11135	Springer
Methodological Innovations https://journals.sagepub.com/home/mio	Sage
Caribbean Journal of Mixed Methods Research https://www.uwipress.com/journals/the-caribbean-journal-of-mixed-methods-research/	The University of the West Indies Press
BMC Medical Research Methodology https://bmcmedresmethodol.biomedcentral.com/	BMC, part of Springer Nature
The Annals of Mixed Methods Research https://www.jstage.jst.go.jp/browse/ammr/-char/en	The Japan Society of Mixed Methods Research
International Journal of Social Research Methodology https://www.tandfonline.com/toc/tsrm20/current	Taylor & Francis Online

(continues)

Journal	Publisher
MMR protocol papers	
BMC Health Services Research https://bmchealthservres.biomedcentral.com/	BMC, part of Springer Nature
BMJ Open https://bmjopen.bmj.com/	BMJ Journals
Implementation Science https://implementationscience.biomedcentral.com/	BMC, part of Springer Nature
JMIR Research Protocols https://www.researchprotocols.org/	JMIR Publications
Business	
Qualitative Research in Accounting & Management https://www.emerald.com/insight/publication/issn/1176-6093	Emerald Publishing
Management Research Review https://www.emeraldgrouppublishing.com/journal/mrr	Emerald Publishing

Note. APA = American Psychological Association; BMJ = British Medical Journal; JMIR = Journal of Medical Internet Research; MMR = mixed methods research; BMC = BioMed Central.

Appendix C

UNIVERSITY PROGRAMS IN MIXED METHODS RESEARCH

Drexel University: Creative Art Therapy and School of Education
Fresno State University: Certificate of Advanced Study in Research Methods
George Mason University: Research Methods Graduate Certificate
Harvard University-Harvard Catalyst
International Congress of Qualitative Inquiry
Johns Hopkins Bloomberg School of Public Health: Mixed Methods Research
   Training Program for the Health Sciences
Ohio University, Certificate in Mixed methods Research Online
Pokhara University (Nepal)
Southwest Mixed Methods Conference
Stanford University
Texas Tech University Foundations of Mixed Methods Research
The University of Alabama at Birmingham Graduate Certificate in Applications
   of Mixed Methods Research
University of Alberta
University of Auckland (New Zealand)
University of Edinburgh
University of Massachusetts-Boston
University of Michigan Mixed Methods Program, Online Certificate Program
   in Mixed Methods Research, School of Social Work
University of Nebraska-Lincoln: Certificate Mixed Methods Research
University of Nevada, Las Vegas: Advanced Graduate Certificate in Mixed
   Methods Research
University of North Carolina
University of West Indies
University of the Western Cape (South Africa)

Glossary

abduction The process of going back and forth between deduction (examining data) and induction (inferences based on the data).

aims The research objectives of a mixed methods research study.

analysis integration When one type of data analysis influences another type of data analysis (crossover analysis).

a posteriori The process of using codes derived from the data as opposed to a priori codes which are decided before coding data.

arts-based mixed methods research Use of arts activities from drama, visual arts, music, and/or dance to help people access and express unconscious thoughts and feelings. It can include the artwork as a data set.

arts therapy mixed methods research Incorporation of techniques in the creative arts therapies as an intervention to improve physiological and psychological outcomes of an experimental mixed methods design.

baseline data Statistical comparison of measured changes, rates, or performances before and after an intervention in a mixed methods experimental design.

between-subjects designs Examination of the effects of a treatment/condition across two or more groups (treatment and control group) in a mixed methods experimental design.

case studies Examination of results at the individual level within the wider sample of those who have participated in a randomized controlled trial (RCT) in a mixed methods experimental design.

classical test theory (CTT) Use of factor analysis to examine clusters, or sets of items, and the corresponding total score especially when using a sequential exploratory mixed methods design to create a new or adapt an existing instrument or survey.

codes The smallest conceptual unit of text in a transcription of an interview, focus group, or other recorded event, that can be used to sort, organize, and compare large volumes of qualitative data across persons, groups, or cases.

color-coded joint displays The matching of colored qualitative interview or focus group results with exemplar quotes to the same color boxplot or other type of quantitative results.

complementarity The process of elaborating on one set of results with another set of results.

content analysis A way to make sense out of concepts underlying qualitative data by coding transcribed data.

convergent (or concurrent) mixed methods research designs Incorporation of both quantitative and qualitative data by either prioritizing one data set or giving them equal priority or status in the project.

counterbalanced designs The provision of a treatment/intervention to all groups but in different orders in a mixed methods experimental design.

creative joint displays Use of novel figures to tie the significance of statistical results to corresponding thematic results to theories.

culturally responsive or culturally sensitive techniques Responding to the needs, experiences, and perspectives of people from diverse backgrounds who may experience marginalization in society, or have been excluded from past research studies, to expand the use and application of mixed methods research.

cultural relevance The ways in which researchers recognize, value, and purposefully include people's Indigenous knowledge and cultural experiences in multiple ways, such as in the cocreation of research processes, tools, protocols, and metrics from a community's perspective, not just from a researcher's or research team's perspective.

data collection integration Allowing people to opt into data collection. It can be particularly important when researchers aim to include minoritized communities and want to design culturally sensitive studies.

data saturation The point when sufficient data are obtained/collected to explain a phenomenon or concept.

data transformation method The process of converting either a quantitative into a quantitative data set or vice versa.

development Using a data set (e.g., qualitative interviews) to develop an instrument or survey.

dialogic relationship The way that mixed methods results can be compared and either confirm or disconfirm important aspects.

educational studies Studies that highlight the utility value of the research for learners, teachers, instruction, and curriculum, and other ways to enhance the educational processes and outcomes.

emancipation See liberation.

ethics Treatment according to moral principles or values of various persons involved in the mixed methods study: research team members, community members, and organizations like schools, and human subjects treatment.

expansion The extension of one phase with another phase in a mixed methods study.

experimental designs Investigation of the effects of an activity, treatment, medicine, or other type of planned intervention embedded in a mixed methods design, also called a "complex" design.

experiments Research studies that measure treatment or intervention effects by manipulating an independent variable and measuring a dependent variable, wherein individual participants are randomly selected and then randomly assigned to either a treatment/intervention group or a control group that does not receive that treatment/intervention.

explanatory sequential mixed method designs Designs that often pair a survey (quantitative) followed by an interview (qualitative).

exploratory sequential mixed methods designs Designs that often pair interviews or focus groups first as a core approach to developing or altering a survey or instrument.

focus groups A qualitative method used for group discussion on a specific topic to get diverse, heterogeneous perspectives represented in a mixed methods study.

grants Competitive funding programs designed to support mixed methods research either from private foundations or public agencies.

grounded theory mixed methods research Research that starts with qualitative data collection that can be tested quantitatively to drive new theory.

hypotheses Statements that can be proved or disproved through the collection of quantitative data in a mixed methods research project.

initiation The process of addressing discrepant or contradictory evidence by deriving new variables or other data-driven approaches to the research under investigation.

integration The process of demonstrating novel associations across quantitative and qualitative elements and is an important element in mixed methods publications.

intersectionality The multiple, overlapping personal identities including race, gender, ethnicity, sexuality, ability, and socioeconomic status, and how these identities affect one's worldview, perspectives, and behaviors.

interviews The most common qualitative method used in mixed methods research to engage study participants in questions to unearth descriptions of thoughts, feelings, worldviews, and experiences.

joint display Graphical displays that represent the overlap or divergence of the qualitative and quantitative results.

liberation Addressing silenced, oppressed, or marginalized voices in mixed methods research, especially in instances when social truths might otherwise be dismissed or ignored as valid.

member checking Addressing the process of sharing transcriptions, data analysis, and/or results with participants to ensure fairness and ethics in the representation of voices and narratives to the wider public.

mixed methods research The intentional design, combination and integration of at least one qualitative and quantitative research method into a comprehensive research project that incorporates multiple ways of making sense of the social world.

multiple truth orientation A philosophy undergirding mixed methods research to value multiple aspects of the social world.

multitrait multimethod research (MTMM) The examination of several separate quantitative operational definitions of one construct. Multimethod studies may use multiple qualitative strands, multiple quantitative strands, or both.

narrative qualitative research Research that relies on stories gained through autobiography, journaling, writing, and/or interviews.

observations Field research observing people's behaviors either through complete participation or nonparticipation using notes, videos, or a guided rubric, and then subjected to either qualitative or quantitative analyses.

parallel designs Designs where qualitative and quantitative data are collected at the same time. Also referred to as convergent mixed methods designs.

participatory research activities Engagement of study participants in multiple phases of a mixed methods project, including the design, data collection, analyses, presentation, and authorship.

phenomenological research Research that focuses on the temporal unfolding of real events and can be captured either quantitatively or qualitatively in mixed methods research projects.

photovoice research Research that focuses on study participants collecting photographs of important events and experiences to include in the research project.

physiological data Data that represent how the body works during certain tasks, such as actions, percepts, and executive functions, in experimental mixed methods designs.

positionality Demonstrating an awareness of one's position relative to other people's positions and identities in the research study and the research team, typically outlined in a brief statement for possible inclusion in publication.

power analysis The smallest estimated sample size needed for a quantitative strand of a mixed methods study based on significance level, statistical power, and effect size.

pragmatism The practical and optimistic philosophy of science undergirding many mixed methods researchers' work, focusing on promoting social progress, which relates to valuing multiple truths.

preregistration By registering specific hypotheses and posting raw data sets, preregistration helps to prevent false representation of results and foster a climate of open science by specifying hypotheses and uploading data sets.

qualitative research methods Social science research methods that examine, interpret, and account for subjective human experience through talking, writing, discussing, and other modes of artistic expression.

qualitizing The mixed methods strategy of transforming quantitative data into qualitative data, similar to the process of factor analysis, which relies on naming clusters of variables.

quantitative research methods Social science research methods that record numeric ratings representing human experience, thought, behavior and performance and use descriptive and inferential statistical tests to analyze the results.

quantitizing The mixed methods strategy of assigning numerical values to data-derived codes to express the salience or prevalence of that code.

quasi-experimental designs Random assignment of groups rather than random assignment of individual participants to a treatment(s) in mixed methods experimental designs.

random assignment Selecting participants in a random manner to receive treatments in an experiment (used in a mixed methods experiment).

randomized controlled trial (RCT) The random assignment of units to an intervention, policy, or program or to a control group in order to make inferences of causality attributable to that intervention (used in a mixed methods experiment).

random sampling Selecting participants from a certain population using the principle of equal probability for selection (used in a mixed methods experiment).

rationale The specific reason a mixed methods design is needed as opposed to a single study or multi-method study.

Rasch modeling A statistical technique using item response theory that focuses on how people respond to individual items based on item difficulty in a survey, measure, or instrument for the quantitative phase or strand in a mixed methods study.

reflexivity Engaging in reflection on the research process in each stage of research including stating how the researchers' backgrounds influence the research.

reliability Various quantitative measures of consistency, such as Cronbach's alpha, to measure interrater reliability. Internal consistency reliability and test–retest reliability are also forms of quantitative reliability. In qualitative research, reliability is the way in which data are collected and analyzed in a consistent, transparent, and dependable manner.

replication Repetition of prior experiments conducted to clarify the relationships of variables and to extend an experiment with a new condition or adapt the experiment to a new setting and field.

research problem Characterizing the issue to be examined in terms of the larger societal, psychological, educational, or medical problems that make the mixed methods research exigent, timely, and relevant.

research questions Questions to guide the study and the type of data to be collected and analyzed.

results integration Comparison of two separate results sections.

sample size The intended number of participants for a study based on various characteristics (qualitative) or based on calculating statistical power (quantitative). (See power analysis.)

sampling integration Collecting data with subsets of larger samples used in the initial phase of a mixed methods study.

sampling in qualitative research Purposive strategies to form samples based on the criteria of group membership, expertise, and experience, as well as possible demographic features and intersectional identities.

sampling in quantitative research Random sampling techniques that are used to form a group representative of a larger population who will be recruited to participate in a study.

sampling stage The juncture or time during which the sampling occurs for each phase of the mixed methods study.

sequential mixed methods designs Designs using two separate stages of quantitative or qualitative data and then merging results at the end. (See explanatory or exploratory sequential designs.) These designs are considered distinct from experimental mixed methods designs which place the intervention at the heart of the design.

side-by-side tables A type of joint display that presents quantitative and qualitative analyses using columns and rows.

social justice An orientation guiding mixed methods research to serve and help people who have experienced marginalization due to unjust and discriminatory practices.

thematic analysis A qualitative data analysis framework to categorize qualitative data by themes.

theory A set of propositions or conceptual framework that guides the development of mixed methods research questions and/or hypotheses.

transferability The efforts of researchers to learn about findings and then adapt them to a new context.

transformation See liberation.

triangulation A way to deliberately strengthen the use of different methods by comparing results across quantitative and qualitative results in a mixed methods research project and looking for possible connections.

validity in mixed methods research Different ways that rigor can be supported when using both quantitative and qualitative methods: integration, triangulation, complementarity, development, expansion, initiation, liberation, and cultural relevance.

validity in qualitative research The authenticity, veracity, or truth-value of the responses from participants provided in data collection methods and contexts such as interviews, focus groups, observations, archival records, or other qualitative sources.

validity in quantitative research Various computational methods for understanding variance across items.

video-based research Use of computer cameras or videos to document individual or group activities.

W.E.I.R.D. Western, Educated, Industrialized, Rich, Democratic samples used in psychological science. WEIRD samples are referred to when considering how to make the sampling process, criteria, and decision making more inclusive to the actual population as referred to in the U.S. Census demographics, for example.

within-subjects designs Examination of two or more treatments/conditions within each subject/participant in a mixed methods experimental study.

References

Agans, R. P., Deeb-Sossa, N., & Kalsbeek, W. D. (2006). Mexican immigrants and the use of cognitive assessment techniques in questionnaire development. *Hispanic Journal of Behavioral Sciences, 28*(2), 209–230. https://doi.org/10.1177/0739986305285826

Aiello, M., Bismar, D., Casanova, S., Casas, J. M., Chang, D., Chin, J. L., Comas-Diaz, L., Salvo Crane, L., Demir, Z., Garcia, M. A., Hita, L., Leverett, P., Mendez, K., Morse, G. S., shodiya-zeumault, S., O'Leary Sloan, M., Weil, M. C., & Blume, A. W. (2021). Protecting and defending our people: Nakni tushka anowa (The warrior's path) final report. APA Division 45 Warrior's Path Presidential Task Force (2020). *Journal of Indigenous Research, 9*(2021), Article 8. https://doi.org/10.26077/2en0-6610

Akinola, M., & Mendes, W. B. (2008). The dark side of creativity: Biological vulnerability and negative emotions lead to greater artistic creativity. *Personality and Social Psychology Bulletin, 34*(12), 1677–1686. https://doi.org/10.1177/0146167208323933

Akinola, M. C., Kapadia, C., Lu, J. G., & Mason, M. F. (2019). Incorporating physiology into creativity research and practice: The effects of bodily stress responses on creativity in organizations. *The Academy of Management Perspectives, 33*(2), 163–184. https://doi.org/10.5465/amp.2017.0094

Allmark, P., & Machaczek, K. (2018). Realism and pragmatism in a mixed methods study. *Journal of Advanced Nursing, 74*(6), 1301–1309. https://doi.org/10.1111/jan.13523

American Psychological Association. (2020). *Publication manual of the American Psychological Association* (7th ed.). https://doi.org/10.1037/0000165-000

Anguera, M. T., Blanco-Villaseñor, A., Losada, J. L., Sánchez-Algarra, P., & Onwuegbuzie, A. (2018). Revisiting the difference between mixed methods and multimethods: Is it all in the name? *Quality & Quantity: International Journal of Methodology, 52*(6), 2757–2770. https://doi.org/10.1007/s11135-018-0700-2

Antunes, R. P., Sales, C. M. D., & Elliott, R. (2020). The clinical utility of Personal Questionnaire (PQ): A mixed methods study. *Counselling Psychology Quarterly*, *33*(1), 25–45. https://doi.org/10.1080/09515070.2018.1439451

Archibald, M. M. (2016). Investigator triangulation: A collaborative strategy with potential for mixed methods research. *Journal of Mixed Methods Research*, *10*(3), 228–250. https://doi.org/10.1177/1558689815570092

Bacon, C. K. (2020). "It's not really my job": A mixed methods framework for language ideologies, monolingualism, and teaching emergent bilingual learners. *Journal of Teacher Education, 71*(2), 172–187. https://doi.org/10.1177/0022487118783188

Bartholomew, T. T., & Lockard, A. J. (2018). Mixed methods in psychotherapy research: A review of method(ology) integration in psychotherapy science. *Journal of Clinical Psychology, 74*(10), 1687–1709. https://doi.org/10.1002/jclp.22653

Bazeley, P., & Kemp, L. (2012). Mosaics, triangles, and DNA: Metaphors for integrated analysis in mixed methods research. *Journal of Mixed Methods Research, 6*(1), 55–72. https://doi.org/10.1177/1558689811419514

Beck, C. T., Eaton, C. M., & Gable, R. K. (2016). Vicarious posttraumatic growth in labor and delivery nurses. *Journal of Obstetric, Gynecologic, and Neonatal Nursing, 45*(6), 801–812. https://doi.org/10.1016/j.jogn.2016.07.008

Bennett, A. A., Gabriel, A. S., & Calderwood, C. (2020). Examining the interplay of micro-break durations and activities for employee recovery: A mixed-methods investigation. *Journal of Occupational Health Psychology, 25*(2), 126–142. https://doi.org/10.1037/ocp0000168

Bergman, M. M. (2010). Hermeneutic content analysis: Textual and audiovisual analyses within a mixed methods framework. In A. Tashakkori & C. Teddlie (Eds.), *Sage handbook of mixed methods in social and behavioral research* (pp. 379–396). Sage. https://doi.org/10.4135/9781506335193.n16

Bernstein, R. J. (1988). *Beyond objectivism and relativism: Science, hermeneutics, and praxis*. University of Pennsylvania Press.

Bishop, F. L. (2015). Using mixed methods research designs in health psychology: An illustrated discussion from a pragmatist perspective. *British Journal of Health Psychology, 20*(1), 5–20. https://doi.org/10.1111/bjhp.12122

Bourdieu, P., & Wacquant, L. J. D. (1992). *An invitation to reflexive sociology*. The University of Chicago Press.

Bradt, J., Potvin, N., Kesslick, A., Shim, M., Radl, D., Schriver, E., Gracely, E. J., & Komarnicky-Kocher, L. T. (2015). The impact of music therapy versus music medicine on psychological outcomes and pain in cancer patients: A mixed methods study. *Supportive Care in Cancer, 23*(5), 1261–1271. https://doi.org/10.1007/s00520-014-2478-7

Brett, J. A., Heimendinger, J., Boender, C., Morin, C., & Marshall, J. A. (2002). Using ethnography to improve intervention design. *American Journal of Health Promotion, 16*(6), 331–340. https://doi.org/10.4278/0890-1171-16.6.331

Brewer, J., & Hunter, A. (2006). *Foundations in multimethod research: Synthesizing styles*. Sage Publications. https://doi.org/10.4135/9781412984294

Brown, J. B., Ryan, B. L., Thorpe, C., Markle, E. K. R., Hutchison, B., & Glazier, R. H. (2015). Measuring teamwork in primary care: Triangulation of qualitative and quantitative data. *Families, Systems, & Health, 33*(3), 193–202. https://doi.org/10.1037/fsh0000109

Bryman, A. (2007). The research question in social research: What is its role? *International Journal of Social Research Methodology, 10*(1), 5–20. https://doi.org/10.1080/13645570600655282

Bustamante, C. (2019). TPACK and teachers of Spanish: Development of a theory-based joint display in a mixed methods research case study. *Journal of Mixed Methods Research, 13*(2), 163–178. https://doi.org/10.1177/1558689817712119

Cabrera, N. L. (2011). Using a sequential exploratory mixed-method design to examine racial hyperprivilege in higher education. *New Directions for Institutional Research, 2011*(151), 77–91. https://doi.org/10.1002/ir.400

Campbell, D. T., & Fiske, D. W. (1959). Convergent and discriminant validation by the multitrait–multimethod matrix. *Psychological Bulletin, 56*(2), 81–105. https://doi.org/10.1037/h0046016

Campbell, D. T., & Stanley, J. C. (1966). *Experimental and quasi-experimental designs for research*. Rand McNally.

Carroll, L. J., & Rothe, J. P. (2010). Levels of reconstruction as complementarity in mixed methods research: A social theory-based conceptual framework for integrating qualitative and quantitative research. *International Journal of Environmental Research and Public Health, 7*(9), 3478–3488. https://doi.org/10.3390/ijerph7093478

Carson, S. H., Peterson, J. B., & Higgins, D. (2005). Reliability, validity, and factor structure of the Creative Achievement Questionnaire. *Creativity Research Journal, 17*(1), 37–50. https://doi.org/10.1207/s15326934crj1701_4

Choi, J., Lee, S. E., Choi, S., Kang, B., Jim, S. H., Bae, J., Tate, J. A., & Son, Y-J. (2022). Integration of visual thinking strategies to undergraduate health assessment course: A mixed-method feasibility study. *Nurse Education Today, 113*, Article 105374. https://doi.org/10.1016/j.nedt.2022.105374

Cillessen, A. H. N., & Marks, P. E. L. (2017). Methodological choices in peer nomination research. *New Directions for Child and Adolescent Development, 2017*(157), 21–44. https://doi.org/10.1002/cad.20206

Collins, K. M. T., Onwuegbuzie, A. J., & Johnson, R. B. (2012). Securing a place at the table: A review and extension of legitimation criteria for the conduct of mixed research. *American Behavioral Scientist, 56*(6), 849–865. https://doi.org/10.1177/0002764211433799

Connor, K., & Davidson, J. (2003). Development of a new resilience scale: The Connor-Davidson Resilience Scale (CD-RISC). *Depression and Anxiety, 18*, 76–82. https://doi.org/10.1002/da.10113

Cook, T. D., & Campbell, D. T. (1979). *Quasi-experimentation: Design and analysis issues for field settings*. Rand McNally.

Cooper, J. N., & Hall, J. (2016). Understanding Black male student athletes' experiences at a historically Black college/university: A mixed methods approach. *Journal of Mixed Methods Research, 10*(1), 46–63. https://doi.org/10.1177/1558689814558451

Cram, F., & Mertens, D. M. (2015). Transformative and Indigenous frameworks for multimethod and mixed methods research. In S. N. Hesse-Biber & R. B. Johnson (Eds.), *The Oxford handbook of multimethod and mixed methods research inquiry* (pp. 91–109). Oxford University Press.

Creamer, E. G. (2018). *An introduction to fully integrated mixed methods research*. Sage. https://doi.org/10.4135/9781071802823

Creamer, E. G. (2022). *Advancing grounded theory with mixed methods*. Routledge.

Creswell, J. W. (1995). *Research design: Qualitative and quantitative approaches*. Sage.

Creswell, J. W. (2003). *Research design: Qualitative, quantitative, and mixed methods approaches* (2nd ed.). Sage.

Creswell, J. W. (2022). *A concise introduction to mixed methods research* (2nd ed.). Sage.

Creswell, J. W., Klassen, A. C., Plano Clark, V. L., & Smith, K. C. (2011). *Best practices for mixed methods research in the health sciences*. Office of Behavioral and Social Sciences Research (OBSSR), National Institutes of Health. https://obssr.od.nih.gov/sites/obssr/files/Best_Practices_for_Mixed_Methods_Research.pdf

Creswell, J. W., & Plano Clark, V. L. (2018). *Designing and conducting mixed methods research* (3rd ed.). Sage.

Creswell, J. W., Shope, R., Clark, V. L. P., & Green, D. O. (2006). How interpretive qualitative research extends mixed methods research. *Research in the Schools, 13*(1), 1–11.

Cyr, K. S., Liu, J. J. W., Cramm, H., Nazarov, A., Hunt, R., Forchuk, C., Deda, E., & Richardson, J. D. (2022). "You can't un-ring the bell": A mixed methods approach to understanding veteran and family perspectives of recovery from military-related posts traumatic stress disorder. *BMC Psychiatry, 22*, Article 37. https://doi.org/10.1186/s12888-021-03622-3

Dattilio, F. M., Edwards, D. J. A., & Fishman, D. B. (2010). Case studies within a mixed methods paradigm: Toward a resolution of the alienation between researcher and practitioner in psychotherapy research. *Psychotherapy: Theory, Research, Practice, Training, 47*(4), 427–441. https://doi.org/10.1037/a0021181

Davelaar, E. J., Barnby, J. M., Almasi, S., & Eatough, V. (2018). Differential subjective experiences in learners and non-learners in frontal alpha neurofeedback: Piloting a mixed-method approach. *Frontiers in Human Neuroscience, 12*, Article 402. https://doi.org/10.3389/fnhum.2018.00402

David, S. L., Hitchcock, J. H., Ragan, B., Brooks, G., & Starkey, C. (2018). Mixing interviews and Rasch modeling: Demonstrating a procedure used to develop and instrument that measures trust. *Journal of Mixed Methods Research, 12*(1), 75–94. https://doi.org/10.1177/1558689815624586

Davidov, D., Bush, H. M., Clear, E. R., & Coker, A. L. (2020). Using a multiphase mixed methods triangulation design to measure bystander intervention components and dose of violence prevention programs on college campuses. *Journal of Family Violence, 35*(6), 551–562. https://doi.org/10.1007/s10896-019-00108-5

DeCuir-Gunby, J. T. (2020). Using critical race mixed methodology to explore the experiences of African Americans in education. *Educational Psychologist, 55*(4), 244–255. https://doi.org/10.1080/00461520.2020.1793762

Dehghan-nayeri, N., Shali, M., Vaezi, A., Navabi, N., & Ghaffari, F. (2019). Cardiac patients' beliefs about their illness and treatment: A sequential exploratory mixed methods design. *Medical Journal of the Islamic Republic of Iran, 33*(1), 591–596. https://doi.org/10.47176/mjiri.33.98

de Jong, L., Plöthner, M., Stahmeyer, J. T., Eberhard, S., Zeidler, J., & Damm, K. (2019). Informal and formal care preferences and expected willingness of providing elderly care in Germany: Protocol for a mixed-methods study. *BMJ Open, 9*(1), Article e023253. https://doi.org/10.1136/bmjopen-2018-023253

Denzin, N. K. (1978). *The research act: A theoretical introduction to sociological methods*. McGraw-Hill.

de Visser, R. O., & McDonnell, E. J. (2012). 'That's OK. He's a guy': A mixed-methods study of gender double-standards for alcohol use. *Psychology & Health, 27*(5), 618–639. https://doi.org/10.1080/08870446.2011.617444

Dewey, J. (1967–1991). *The collected works of John Dewey* (J. A. Boydston, Ed.). Southern Illinois University Press.

Dillman, D. A. (2000). *Mail and internet surveys: The tailored design method* (2nd ed.). John Wiley and Sons.

Edmonson, S., & Irby, B. (2008). *Ten tips for producing a top qualitative research study*. Pearson.

Fan, X. (1998). Item response and classical test theory: An empirical comparison of their item/person statistics. *Educational and Psychological Measurement, 58*(3), 357–381. https://doi.org/10.1177/0013164498058003001

Feilzer, M. Y. (2010). Doing mixed methods research pragmatically: Implications for the rediscovery of pragmatism as a research paradigm. *Journal of Mixed Methods Research, 4*(1), 6–16. https://doi.org/10.1177/1558689809349691

Fentaw, Y., Moges, B. T., & Ismail, S. M. (2022). Academic procrastination behavior among public university students. *Education Research International, 2022*, Article 1277866. https://doi.org/10.1155/2022/1277866

Fetters, M. D. (2020). *The mixed methods research workbook: Activities for designing, implementing, and publishing projects*. Sage.

Fetters, M. D., Curry, L. A., & Creswell, J. W. (2013). Achieving integration in mixed methods designs—Principles and practices. *Health Services Research, 48*(6 Pt 2), 2134–2156. https://doi.org/10.1111/1475-6773.12117

Fitzpatrick, K. R. (2016). Points of convergence in music education: The use of data labels as a strategy for mixed methods integration. *Journal of Mixed Methods Research, 10*(3), 273–291. https://doi.org/10.1177/1558689814560264

Flick, U. (2018). *Doing triangulation and mixed methods.* Sage. https://doi.org/10.4135/9781529716634

Flick, U., Garms-Homolová, V., Herrmann, W. J., Kuck, J., & Röhnsch, G. (2012). "I can't prescribe something just because someone asks for it": Using mixed methods in the framework of triangulation. *Journal of Mixed Methods Research, 6*(2), 97–110. https://doi.org/10.1177/1558689812437183

Fowler, F. J., Jr. (2009). *Survey research methods* (4th ed.). Sage.

Gay, L. R., Mills, G. E., & Airasian, P. (2009). *Educational research: Competencies for analysis and applications.* Pearson.

Geertz, C. (1973). *The interpretation of cultures: Selected essays.* Basic Books.

Gieser, L., & Stein, M. I. (Eds.). (1999). *Evocative images: The Thematic Apperception Test and the art of projection.* American Psychological Association. https://doi.org/10.1037/10334-000

Glaser, B., & Strauss, A. (1967). *The discovery of grounded theory: Strategies for qualitative research.* Aldine.

Glogowska, M. (2011). Paradigms, pragmatism and possibilities: Mixed-methods research in speech and language therapy. *International Journal of Language & Communication Disorders, 46*(3), 251–260. https://doi.org/10.3109/13682822.2010.507614

Goodwin, J., Lecouturier, J., Basu, A., Colver, A., Crombie, S., Smith, J., Howel, D., McColl, E., Parr, J. R., Kolehmainen, N., Roberts, A., Miller, K., & Cadwgan, J. (2018). Standing frames for children with cerebral palsy: A mixed-methods feasibility study. *Health Technology Assessment, 22*(50), 1–232. https://doi.org/10.3310/hta22500

Graziano, A. M., & Raulin, M. L. (2013). *Research methods: A process of inquiry* (8th ed.). Pearson.

Green, S. B., & Salkind, N. J. (2017). *Using SPSS for Windows and Macintosh: Analyzing and understanding the data* (8th ed.). Pearson.

Greene, J. (2007). *Mixed methods in social inquiry.* Jossey-Bass.

Greene, J., & McClintock, C. (1985). Triangulation in evaluation: Design and analysis issues. *Evaluation Review, 9*(5), 523–545. https://doi.org/10.1177/0193841X8500900501

Greene, J. C., Caracelli, V. J., & Graham, W. F. (1989). Toward a conceptual framework for mixed-method evaluation designs. *Educational Evaluation and Policy Analysis, 11*(3), 255–274. https://doi.org/10.3102/01623737011003255

Guetterman, T. C., Fabregues, S., & Sakakibara, R. (2021). Visuals in joint displays to represent integration in mixed methods research: A methodological review. *Methods in Psychology, 5,* Article 100080. https://doi.org/10.1016/j.metip.2021.100080

Guilford, J. P. (1966). Intelligence: 1965 model. *American Psychologist, 21*(1), 20–26. https://doi.org/10.1037/h0023296

Gurven, M. D. (2018). Broadening horizons: Sample diversity and socioecological theory are essential to the future of psychological science. *PNAS: Proceedings of the National Academy of Sciences of the United States of America, 115*(45), 11420–11427. https://doi.org/10.1073/pnas.1720433115

Hamed, O., Jabbad, H. H., Saadah, O. I., Al Ahwal, M. S., & Al-Sayes, F. M. (2018). An explanatory mixed methods study on the validity and validation of students' assessment results in the undergraduate surgery course. *Medical Teacher, 40*(Suppl. 1), S56–S67. https://doi.org/10.1080/0142159X.2018.1465181

Hancock, A., Weeks, A. D., Furber, C., Campbell, M., & Lavender, T. (2021). The Recognition of Excessive blood loss At ChildbirTh (REACT) study: A two-phase exploratory, sequential mixed methods inquiry using focus groups, interviews and a pilot, randomised crossover study. *BJOG, 128*(11), 1843–1854. https://doi.org/10.1111/1471-0528.16735

Haraway, D. (1988). Situated knowledges: The science question in feminism and the privilege of partial perspectives. *Feminist Studies, 14*(3), 575–599. https://doi.org/10.2307/3178066

Hass, R., Katz-Buonincontro, J., & Reiter-Palmon, R. (2016). Disentangling creative mindsets from creative self-efficacy and creative identity: Do people hold fixed and growth theories of creativity? *Psychology of Aesthetics, Creativity, and the Arts, 10*(4), 436–446. https://doi.org/10.1037/aca0000081

Hatta, T., Narita, K., Yanagihara, K., Ishiguro, H., Murayama, T., & Yokode, M. (2020). Crossover mixed analysis in a convergent mixed mehods design used to investigate clinical dialogues about cancer treatment in the Japanese context. *Journal of Mixed Methods Research, 14*(1), 84–109. https://doi.org/10.1177/1558689818792793

Hesse-Biber, S. (2012). Feminist approaches to triangulation: Uncovering subjugated knowledge and fostering social change in mixed methods research. *Journal of Mixed Methods Research, 6*(2), 137–146. https://doi.org/10.1177/1558689812437184

Hesse-Biber, S. N. (2010). Feminist approaches to mixed methods research: Linking theory to praxis. In A. Tashakkori & C. Teddlie (Eds.), *Sage handbook of mixed methods in social and behavioral research* (pp. 169–192). Sage. https://doi.org/10.4135/9781506335193.n7

Heyvaert, M., Hannes, K., & Onghena, P. (2017). *Using mixed methods research synthesis for literature reviews.* Sage. https://doi.org/10.4135/9781506333243

Hitchcock, J. H., Nastasi, B. K., Dai, D. Y., Newman, J., Jayasena, A., Bernstein-Moore, R., Sarkar, S., & Varjas, K. (2005). Illustrating a mixed-method approach for validating culturally specific constructs. *Journal of School Psychology, 43*(3), 259–278. https://doi.org/10.1016/j.jsp.2005.04.007

Howe, K. R. (2012). Mixed methods, triangulation, and causal explanation. *Journal of Mixed Methods Research, 6*(2), 89–96. https://doi.org/10.1177/1558689812437187

Hume, C., Salmon, J., & Ball, K. (2005). Children's perceptions of their home and neighborhood environments, and their association with objectively measured physical activity: A qualitative and quantitative study. *Health Education Research, 20*(1), 1–13. https://doi.org/10.1093/her/cyg095

Huynh, K., & Farhadi Langroudi, K. (2016). *Intersectionalities in psychology: Intersections of race, sexual orientation, and gender* [Webinar]. American Psychological Association of Graduate Students' Committee on Sexual Orientation and Gender Diversity. https://www.apa.org/apags/governance/subcommittees/intersectionalities-in-psychology.pdf

Institute of Education Sciences. (2015). Mixed methods in education research. National Center for Education Research. https://files.eric.ed.gov/fulltext/ED580319.pdf

Jabine, T. B., Straf, M. L., Tanur, J. M., & Tourageau, R. (1984). *Cognitive aspects of survey methodology: Building a bridge between disciplines.* The National Academies Press. https://doi.org/10.17226/930

Jaccard, J., & Jacoby, J. (2010). *Theory construction and model-building skills: A practical guide for social scientists.* Guilford Press.

Jafer, M., Crutzen, R., Ibrahim, A., Moafa, I., Zaylaee, H., Ajeely, M., van den Borne, B., Zanza, A., Testarelli, L., & Patil, S. (2021). Using the exploratory sequential mixed methods design to investigate dental patients' perceptions and needs concerning oral cancer information, examination, prevention and behavior. *International Journal of Environmental Research and Public Health, 18*(14), Article 7562. https://doi.org/10.3390/ijerph18147562

James, W. (1981). *Pragmatism* (B. Kuklick, Ed.). Hackett.

Jick, T. D. (1979). Mixing qualitative and quantitative methods: Triangulation in action. *Administrative Science Quarterly, 24*(4), 602–611. https://doi.org/10.2307/2392366

Johnson, B., & Christensen, L. (2008). *Educational research: Quantitative, qualitative, and mixed methods* (3rd ed.). Sage.

Johnson, R. E., Grove, A. L., & Clarke, A. (2019). Pillar integration process: A joint display technique to integrate data in mixed methods research. *Journal of Mixed Methods Research, 13*(3), 301–320. https://doi.org/10.1177/1558689817743108

Kadushin, C., Hecht, S., Sasson, T., & Saxe, L. (2008). Triangulation and mixed methods design: Practicing what we preach in the evaluation of an Israel experience educational program. *Field Methods, 20*(1), 46–65. https://doi.org/10.1177/1525822X07307426

Karam, F. J., Kibler, A. K., Johnson, H. E., & Molloy Elreda, L. (2020). Identity, positionality, and peer social networks: A case study of an adolescent refugee background student. *Journal of Language, Identity, and Education, 19*(3), 208–223. https://doi.org/10.1080/15348458.2019.1655427

Katz-Buonincontro, J. (2022). *How to interview and conduct focus groups.* American Psychological Association. https://doi.org/10.1037/0000299-000

Katz-Buonincontro, J., Anderson, R., & Manalang, V. (2020). Understanding the mechanisms and prevalence of creative engagement in theatre-based instruction. *Methods in Psychology, 2*, 100013. https://doi.org/10.1016/jmetip.2019.100013

Keegan, S. (2008). Projective techniques. In L. M. Given (Ed.), *The Sage encyclopedia of qualitative research* (pp. 686–688). Sage.

Keown, E. L. (2013). *The impact of an art-based media literacy curriculum on the leadership self-efficacy of adolescent girls* [Unpublished doctoral dissertation]. Edgewood College.

Keshavarzian, K., Nadrian, H., & Mohammadpoorasl, A. (2020). Development of a Cigarette Smoking Obscenity Scale (CSOS) in adolescents: An exploratory sequential mixed method design. *Health Promotion Perspectives, 10*(2), 129–134. https://doi.org/10.34172/hpp.2020.21

Kim, Y., & Lim, J. H. (2013). Gendered socialization with an embodied agent: Creating a social and affable mathematics learning environment for middle-grade females. *Journal of Educational Psychology, 105*(4), 1164–1174. https://doi.org/10.1037/a0031027

Kish, L. (1965). *Survey sampling*. John Wiley & Sons.

Knaust, T., Felnhofer, A., Kothgassner, O. D., Reinke, M., Browning, M., Höllmer, H., & Schulz, H. (2022). Nature videos for PTSD: Protocol for a mixed-methods feasibility study. *European Journal of Psychotraumatology, 13*(2), Article 2101765. https://doi.org/10.1080/20008198.2022.2101765

Lacy, A. M. P., Eason, C. M., Stearns, R. L., & Casa, D. J. (2021). Secondary school administrators' knowledge and perceptions of the athletic training profession, part 1: Specific considerations for athletic directors. *Journal of Athletic Training, 56*(9), 1018–1028. https://doi.org/10.4085/54-20

Lennon, R. P., Fraleigh, R., Van Scoy, L. J., Keshaviah, A., Hu, X. C., Snyder, B. L., Miller, E. L., Calo, W. A., Zgierska, A. E., & Griffin, C. (2021). Developing and testing an automated qualitative assistant (AQUA) to support qualitative analysis. *Family Medicine and Community Health, 9*(Suppl. 1). https://doi.org/10.1136/fmch-2021-001287

Levitt, H. M. (2020). *Reporting qualitative research in psychology: How to meet APA style journal article reporting standards* (Rev. ed.). American Psychological Association. https://doi.org/10.1037/0000179-000

Levitt, H. M., Bamberg, M., Creswell, J. W., Frost, D. M., Josselson, R., & Suárez-Orozco, C. (2018). Journal article reporting standards for qualitative primary, qualitative meta-analytic, and mixed methods research in psychology: The APA Publications and Communications Board task force report. *American Psychologist, 73*(1), 26–46. https://doi.org/10.1037/amp0000151

Li, C., & Xu, J. (2019). Trait emotional intelligence and classroom emotions: A positive psychology investigation and intervention among Chinese EFL learners. *Frontiers in Psychology, 10*, Article 2453. https://doi.org/10.3389/fpsyg.2019.02453

Lincoln, Y. S., & Guba, E. G. (1985). *Naturalistic inquiry*. Sage.

Liu, Q., Wang, Y., Tang, Q., & Liu, Z. (2020). Do you feel the same as I do? Differences in virtual reality technology experience and acceptance between elderly adults and college students. *Frontiers in Psychology, 11*(1), Article 573673. https://doi.org/10.3389/fpsyg.2020.573673

Lynam, T., Damayanti, R., Rialine Titaley, C., Suharno, N., Bradley, M., & Krentel, A. (2020). Reframing integration for mixed methods research. *Journal of Mixed Methods Research, 14*(3), 336–357. https://doi.org/10.1177/1558689819879352

MacLin, M. K. (2020). *Experimental design in psychology: A case approach* (9th ed.). Routledge. https://doi.org/10.4324/9780367808280

Manansingh, S., Tatum, S. L., & Morote, E.-S. (2019). Effects of relaxation techniques on nursing students' academic stress and test anxiety. *The Journal of Nursing Education, 58*(9), 534–537. https://doi.org/10.3928/01484834-20190819-07

Mantzios, M., & Giannou, K. (2018). When did coloring books become mindful? Exploring the effectiveness of a novel method of mindfulness-guided instructions for coloring books to increase mindfulness and decrease anxiety. *Frontiers in Psychology, 9*(56), Article 56. https://doi.org/10.3389/fpsyg.2018.00056

McCrudden, M. T., & McTighe, E. M. (2019). Implementing integration in an explanatory sequential mixed methods study of belief bias about climate change with high school students. *Journal of Mixed Methods Research, 13*(3), 381–400. https://doi.org/10.1177/1558689818762576

McDonnell, D., Vasiliou, V. S., Lonergan, E., & Moore, P. (2022). Psychologists' experiences who managed waitlists in mental-health services during the COVID-19 lockdown: A mixed-method study. *European Journal of Psychology Open, 81*(2), 47–56. https://doi.org/10.1024/2673-8627/a000024

McLean, C. P., Miller, M. L., Dondanville, K. A., Rauch, S. A. M., Yarvis, J. S., Wright, E. C., Hall-Clark, B. N., Fina, B. A., Litz, B. T., Mintz, J., Young-McCaughan, S., Peterson, A. L., & Foa, E. B. (2022). Perceptions and experiences of web-prolonged exposure for posttraumatic stress disorder: A mixed-methods study. *Psychological Trauma: Theory, Research, Practice, and Policy*. Advance online publication. https://doi.org/10.1037/tra0001124

McMahon, J. M., Simmons, J., Haberer, J. E., Mannheimer, S., Leblanc, N. M., Torres, L., Quiles, R., Aedo, G., Javier, A., Braksmajer, A., Harriman, G., Trabold, N., Pouget, E. R., Kurth, A., Smith, M. D. R., Brasch, J., Podsiadly, E. J., & Anderson, P. L. (2021). The Magnetic Couples Study: Protocol for a mixed methods prospective cohort study of HIV-serodifferent heterosexual couples' perspectives and use of pre-exposure prophylaxis (PrEP). *BMJ Open*, Article e048993. https://doi.org/10.1136/bmjopen-2021-048993

McNair, D., Lorr, M., & Droppleman, L. (1971). *Manual for the profile of mood states*. EdITS.

Mehra, K., Hawke, L. D., Watson, P., Sheikhan, N. Y., Leroux, E., & Henderson, J. (2021). Youth perspectives on seeking psychotherapy: A concurrent mixed methods study. *Journal of the Canadian Academy of Child and Adolescent Psychiatry, 30*(31), 165–176.

Merriam, S. B. (2009). *Qualitative research: A guide to design and implementation.* John Wiley & Sons.

Mertens, D. M. (2003). Mixed methods and the politics of human research: The transformative-emancipatory perspective. In A. Tashakkori & C. Teddlie (Eds.), *Handbook of mixed methods in social and behavioral research* (pp. 135–164). Sage.

Mertler, C. (2012). *Action research: Improving schools and empowering educators* (3rd ed.). Sage.

Miles, M., & Huberman, D. M. (1994). *Qualitative data analysis: A sourcebook of new methods* (2nd ed.). Sage.

Morgan, D. L. (2007). Paradigms lost and pragmatism regained: Methodological implications of combining qualitative and quantitative methods. *Journal of Mixed Methods Research, 1*(1), 48–76. https://doi.org/10.1177/2345678906292462

Morgan, D. L. (2008). Snowball sampling. In L. M. Given (Ed.), *The Sage encyclopedia of qualitative research methods* (pp. 815–816). Sage.

Morse, J. M. (1991). Approaches to qualitative–quantitative methodological triangulation. *Nursing Research, 40*(2), 120–123.

Morse, J. M. (2010). Issues in qualitatively-driven mixed-method designs: Walking through a mixed-methods project. In S. Hesse-Biber & R. B. Johnson (Eds.), *The Oxford handbook of multimethod and mixed methods research inquiry* (pp. 206–222). Oxford University Press.

Mustanski, B., Coventry, R., Macapagal, K., Arbeit, M. R., & Fisher, C. B. (2017). Sexual and gender minority adolescents' views on HIV research participation and parental permission: A mixed-methods study. *Perspectives on Sexual and Reproductive Health, 49*(2), 111–121. https://doi.org/10.1363/psrh.12027

Myers, K. D., Swars Auslander, S., Smith, S. Z., Smith, M. E., & Fuentes, D. S. (2020). Developing the pedagogical capabilities of elementary mathematics specialists during a K–5 mathematics endorsement program. *Journal of Teacher Education, 71*(2), 261–274. https://doi.org/10.1177/0022487119854437

Nadarzynski, T., Miles, O., Cowie, A., & Ridge, D. (2019). Acceptability of artificial intelligence (AI)-led chatbot services in healthcare: A mixed-methods study. *Digital Health, 5*, 1–12. https://doi.org/10.1177/2055207619871808

Nastasi, B. K., & Hitchcock, J. H. (2016). *Mixed methods research and culture-specific interventions: Program design and evaluation.* Sage. https://doi.org/10.4135/9781483399959

Nastasi, B. K., Hitchcock, J., Sarkar, S., Burkholder, G., Varjas, K., & Jayasena, A. (2007). Mixed methods in intervention research: Theory to adaptation. *Journal of Mixed Methods Research, 1*(2), 164–182. https://doi.org/10.1177/1558689806298181

Newman, I., Lim, J., & Pineda, F. (2013). Mixed methods approach: Its application and development through the use of a table of specifications methodology.

Journal of Mixed Methods Research, 7(3), 243–260. https://doi.org/10.1177/1558689813476922

Nickel, B., Berger, M., Schmidt, P., & Plies, K. (1995). Qualitative sampling in a multi-method survey. *Quality & Quantity, 29*(3), 223–240. https://doi.org/10.1007/BF01101971

Nicol, A. M., & Pexman, P. M. (2010a). *Displaying your findings: A practical guide for creating figures, posters, and presentations* (6th ed.). American Psychological Association.

Nicol, A. M., & Pexman, P. M. (2010b). *Presenting your findings: A practical guide for creating tables* (6th ed.). American Psychological Association.

Nightingale, A. (2006). The nature of gender: Work, gender and environment. *Environment and Planning D: Society & Space, 24*(2), 165–185. https://doi.org/10.1068/d01k

Nunnally, J. C., & Bernstein, I. H. (1994). *Psychometric theory* (3rd ed.). McGraw-Hill.

Nzabonimpa, J. P. (2018). Quantitizing and qualitizing (im-)possibilities in mixed methods research. *Methodological Innovations, 11*(2). https://doi.org/10.1177/2059799118789021

Onwuegbuzie, A. J., Bustamante, R. M., & Nelson, J. A. (2010). Mixed research as a tool for developing quantitative instruments. *Journal of Mixed Methods Research, 4*(1), 56–78. https://doi.org/10.1177/1558689809355805

Onwuegbuzie, A. J., & Johnson, R. B. (Eds.). (2021). *The Routledge reviewer's guide to mixed methods analysis* (pp. 291–304). Routledge Taylor & Francis Group.

Parey, B. (2019). Understanding teachers' attitudes towards the inclusion of children with disabilities in inclusive schools using mixed methods: The case of Trinidad. *Teaching and Teacher Education, 83*, 199–211. https://doi.org/10.1016/j.tate.2019.04.007

Parke, M. R., Tangirala, S., & Hussain, I. (2021). Creating organizational citizens: How and when supervisor- versus peer-led role interventions change organizational citizenship behavior. *Journal of Applied Psychology, 106*(11), 1714–1733. https://doi.org/10.1037/apl0000848

Patton, M. (2002). *Qualitative research and evaluation methods* (3rd ed.). Sage.

Peirce, C. S. (1932–1958). *The collected papers of Charles Sanders Peirce* (C. Hartshorne & P. Weiss, Eds., Vols. 1–6; A. Burks, Ed., Vols. 7–8). Harvard University Press.

Peladeau, N. (2021). Mixing beyond mixed methods: QDA Minder, SimStat, and WordStat. In A. J. Onwuegbuzie & R. B. Johnson (Eds.), *The Routledge reviewer's guide to mixed methods analysis* (pp. 291–304). Routledge Taylor & Francis Group.

Peroff, D. M., Morais, D. B., Seekamp, E., Sills, E., & Wallace, T. (2020). Assessing residents' place attachment to the Guatemalan Maya landscape through mixed methods photo elicitation. *Journal of Mixed Methods Research, 14*(3), 379–402. https://doi.org/10.1177/1558689819845800

Plano Clark, V. P. (2019). Meaningful integration within mixed methods studies: Identifying why, what, when, and how. *Contemporary Educational Psychology, 57*, 106–111. https://doi.org/10.1016/j.cedpsych.2019.01.007

Polachek, A. J., & Wallace, J. E. (2018). The paradox of compassionate work: A mixed-methods study of satisfying and fatiguing experiences of animal health care providers. *Anxiety, Stress, & Coping, 31*(2), 228–243. https://doi.org/10.1080/10615806.2017.1392224

Putnam, L., Wakefield, G., Ji, H., Alper, B., Adderton, D., & Kuchera-Morin, J. (2010). Immersed in unfolding complex systems. In J. Steele & N. Iliinsky (Eds.), *Beautiful visualization: Looking at data through the eyes of experts* (pp. 291–209). O'Reilly.

Rashid, A., & Iguchi, Y. (2019). Female genital cutting in Malaysia: A mixed-methods study. *BMJ Open, 9*(4), Article e025078. https://doi.org/10.1136/bmjopen-2018-025078

Reinhold, A. M., Raile, E. D., Izurieta, C., McEvoy, J., King, H. W., Poole, G. C., Ready, R. C., Bergmann, N. T., & Shanahan, E. A. (2023). Persuasion with precision: Using natural language processing to improve instrument fidelity for risk communication experimental treatments. *Journal of Mixed Methods Research, 17*(4), 373–395. https://doi.org/10.1177/15586898221096934

Rogers, C. R. (1964). Toward a science of the person. In T. W. Wann (Ed.), *Behaviorism and phenomenology: Contrasting bases for modern psychology* (pp. 109–140). The University of Chicago Press.

Rogers, C. R., Okuyemi, K., Paskett, E. D., Thorpe, R. J., Jr., Rogers, T. N., Hung, M., Zickmund, S., Riley, C., & Fetters, M. D. (2019). Study protocol for developing #CuttingCRC: A barbershop-based trial on masculinity barriers to care and colorectal cancer screening uptake among African-American men using an exploratory sequential mixed-methods design. *BMJ Open, 9*(7), Article e030000. https://doi.org/10.1136/bmjopen-2019-030000

Sagor, R. (2005). *The action research guidebook: A four-step process for educators and school teams*. Corwin.

Salkind, N. J. (2017). *Statistics for people who think they hate statistics* (6th ed.). Sage.

Sandelowski, M., Voils, C. I., & Knife, G. (2009). On quantitizing. *Journal of Mixed Methods Research, 3*(3), 208–222. https://doi.org/10.1177/1558689809334210

Schmitt, M. (2006). Conceptual, theoretical, and historical foundations of multi-method assessment. In M. Eid & E. Diener (Eds.), *Handbook of multimethod measurement in psychology* (pp. 9–25). American Psychological Association. https://doi.org/10.1037/11383-002

Schoonenboom, J., & Johnson, R. B. (2017). Wie man ein Mixed Methods-Forschungs-Design konstruiert [How to construct a mixed methods research design]. *Kölner Zeitschrift für Soziologie und Sozialpsychologie, 69*(Suppl. 2), 107–131. https://doi.org/10.1007/s11577-017-0454-1

Segers, E. W., van den Hoogen, A., van Eerden, I. C., Hafsteinsdóttir, T., & Ketelaar, M. (2019). Perspectives of parents and nurses on the content validity of the Family Empowerment Scale for parents of children with a chronic condition: A mixed-methods study. *Child: Care, Health and Development, 45*(1), 111–120. https://doi.org/10.1111/cch.12629

Shadish, W. R., Cook, T. D., & Campbell, D. T. (2002). *Experimental and quasi-experimental designs for generalized causal inference.* Houghton, Mifflin and Company.

Shelton, C. D., Hein, S., & Phipps, K. A. (2020). Resilience and spirituality: A mixed methods exploration of executive stress. *International Journal of Organizational Analysis, 28*(2), 399–416. https://doi.org/10.1108/IJOA-08-2019-1848

Shiyanbola, O. O., Rao, D., Bolt, D., Brown, C., Zhang, M., & Ward, E. (2021). Using an exploratory sequential mixed methods design to adapt an Illness Perception Questionnaire for African Americans with diabetes: The mixed data integration process. *Health Psychology and Behavioral Medicine, 9*(1), 796–817. https://doi.org/10.1080/21642850.2021.1976650

Simões, C., Dibbs, S., & Fisk, R. P. (2005). Managing corporate identity: An internal perspective. *Journal of the Academy of Marketing Science, 33*(2), 153–168. https://doi.org/10.1177/0092070304268920

Singh, S. (2019). What do we know the experiences and outcomes of anti-racist social work education? An empirical case study evidencing contested engagement and transformative learning. *Social Work Education, 38*(5), 631–653. https://doi.org/10.1080/02615479.2019.1592148

Sligo, J. L., Nairn, K. M., & McGee, R. O. (2018). Rethinking integration in mixed methods research using data from different eras: Lessons from a project about teenage vocational behaviour. *International Journal of Social Research Methodology, 21*(1), 63–75. https://doi.org/10.1080/13645579.2017.1321868

Stolz, K. Z. (2017). Milius and mixed methods: Describing and explaining religion and secularity in Switzerland. *Kölner Zeitschrift für Soziologie und Sozialpsychologie, 69*, 361–386. https://doi.org/10.1007/s11577-017-0463-0

Strauss, A. L., & Corbin, J. (1994). Grounded theory methodology: An overview. In N. K. Denzin & Y. S. Lincoln (Eds.), *Handbook of qualitative research* (pp. 273–285). Sage.

Stringer, E. T. (2007). *Action research* (3rd ed.). Sage.

Tanner, D. (2012). *Using statistics to make educational decisions.* Sage.

Tashakkori, A., Johnson, R. B., & Teddlie, C. (2021). *Foundations of mixed methods research: Integrating quantitative and qualitative approaches in social and behavioral sciences* (2nd ed.). Sage.

Tashakkori, A., & Teddlie, C. (1998). *Mixed methodology: Combining qualitative and quantitative approaches.* Sage.

Tebes, J. K. (2012). Philosophical foundations of mixed methods research: Implications for research practice. In L. Jason & D. Glenwick (Eds.), *Methodological approaches to community-based research* (pp. 13–31). American Psychological Association. https://doi.org/10.1037/13492-002

Teddlie, C., & Yu, F. (2007). Mixed methods sampling: A typology with examples. *Journal of Mixed Methods Research, 1*(1), 77–100. https://doi.org/10.1177/1558689806292430

Teye, J. K. (2012). Benefits, challenges, and dynamism of positionalities associated with mixed methods research in developing countries: Evidence from Ghana. *Journal of Mixed Methods Research, 6*(4), 379–391. https://doi.org/10.1177/1558689812453332

Tillman, J. G., Clemence, A. J., & Stevens, J. L. (2011). Mixed methods research design for pragmatic psychoanalytic studies. *Journal of the American Psychoanalytic Association, 59*(5), 1023–1040. https://doi.org/10.1177/0003065111418650

Torrance, H. (2012). Triangulation, respondent validation, and democratic participation in mixed methods research. *Journal of Mixed Methods Research, 6*(2), 111–123. https://doi.org/10.1177/1558689812437185

Trahan, A., & Stewart, D. M. (2013). Toward a pragmatic framework for mixed-methods research in criminal justice and criminology. *Applied Psychology in Criminal Justice, 9*(1), 59–74.

Trochim, W. (1989). An introduction to concept mapping for planning and evaluation. *Evaluation and Program Planning, 12*(1), 1–16. https://doi.org/10.1016/0149-7189(89)90016-5

Tunarosa, A., & Glynn, M. A. (2017). Strategies of integration in mixed methods research: Insights using relational algorithms. *Organizational Research Methods, 20*(2), 224–242. https://doi.org/10.1177/1094428116637197

UNICEF. (2013). *Female genital mutilation/cutting: A statistical overview and exploration of the dynamics of change.* Statistics and Monitoring Section, Division of Policy and Strategy.

Uprichard, E., & Dawney, L. (2019). Data diffraction: Challenging data integration in mixed methods research. *Journal of Mixed Methods Research, 13*(1), 19–32. https://doi.org/10.1177/1558689816674650

U.S. National Institutes of Health. (2022). *Ending structural racism: Data dashboard.* https://www.nih.gov/ending-structural-racism/data-dashboard

Vásquez-Rosati, A., Montefusco-Siegmund, R., López, V., & Cosmelli, D. (2019). Emotional influences on cognitive flexibility depend on individual differences: A combined micro-phenomenological and psychophysiological study. *Frontiers in Psychology, 10*, Article 1138. https://doi.org/10.3389/fpsyg.2019.01138

Vikström, L. (2003). Different sources, different answers: Aspects of women's work in Sundvall, Sweden, 1860–1893. *Interchange, 34*, 241–259.

Webb, E. J., Campbell, D. T., Schwartz, R. D., & Sechrest, L. (1966). *Unobtrusive measures: Nonreactive research in the social sciences.* Rand McNally.

West, C., Usher, K., & Clough, A. R. (2014). Study protocol—Resilience in individuals and families coping with the impacts of alcohol related injuries in remote Indigenous communities: A mixed method study. *BMC Public Health, 14*, Article 479. https://doi.org/10.1186/1471-2458-14-479

West, R., Usher, K., Buettner, P. G., Foster, K., & Stewart, L. (2013). Indigenous Australians' participation in pre-registration tertiary nursing courses: A mixed methods study. *Contemporary Nurse, 46*(1), 123–134. https://doi.org/10.5172/conu.2013.46.1.123

Whewell, W. (1840). *The philosophy of the inductive sciences, founded upon their history* (Vol. 2). John W. Parker.

White, A. M., DeCuir-Gunby, J. T., & Kim, S. (2019). A mixed methods exploration of the relationships between the racial identity, science identity, science self-efficacy, and science achievement of African American students at HBCUs. *Contemporary Educational Psychology, 57*, 54–71. https://doi.org/10.1016/j.cedpsych.2018.11.006

White, K. A. (2014). Development and validation of a tool to measure self-confidence and anxiety in nursing students during clinical decision making. *Journal of Nursing Education, 53*(1), 14–22. https://doi.org/10.3928/01484834-20131118-05

Wiedmaier, B. (2017). Statistical power analysis. In M. Allen (Ed.), *The SAGE encyclopedia of communication research methods*. Sage. https://doi.org/10.4135/9781483381411

Wilson, K., Ramella, K., & Poulos, A. (2022). Building school connectedness through structured recreation during school: A concurrent mixed-methods study. *Journal of School Health, 92*(10), 1013–1021. https://doi.org/10.1111/josh.13222

Wilson, M. (2005). *Constructing measures: An item response modeling approach.* Lawrence Erlbaum Associates.

Wisdom, J. P., & Fetters, M. D. (2015). Funding for mixed methods research: Sources and strategies. In S. N. Hesse-Biber & R. B. Johnson (Eds.), *The Oxford handbook of multimethod and mixed methods research inquiry* (pp. 314–332). Oxford University Press.

Yin, R. K. (2008). *Case study research: Design and methods* (4th ed.). Sage.

Zhang, L., Jackson, H. A., Yang, S., Basham, J. D., Williams, C. H., & Carter, R. A. (2022). Codesigning learning environments guided by the framework of universal design for learning: A case study. *Learning Environments Research, 25*, 379–397. https://doi.org/10.1007/s10984-021-09364-z

Zieber, M., & Sedgwick, M. (2018). Competence, confidence and knowledge retention in undergraduate nursing students—A mixed method study. *Nurse Education Today, 62*, 16–21. https://doi.org/10.1016/j.nedt.2017.12.008

Index

About the Author

Jen Katz-Buonincontro, PhD, MFA, is a professor in the School of Education and Courtesy Professor of Psychology at Drexel University. She teaches research methods, leadership development, and creativity courses. Her sociocognitive research on creative development, identity, and performance in students and educators embraces unique ways of mixing qualitative, quantitative, and arts methods. She also serves as past-president of Division 10, the Society for the Psychology of Aesthetics, Creativity and the Arts, with the American Psychological Association.